Other books by Gary B. Swanson:

The Great Tennis Shoe Dilemma
My Father Owns This Place
Surprise Me!

To order, call 1-800-765-6955.

Visit our website at *www.rhpa.org* for information on other
Review and Herald products.

Gary B. Swanson

THE MOOSE THE GOOSE AND THE KINGDOM OF GOD

REVIEW AND HERALD® PUBLISHING ASSOCIATION
HAGERSTOWN, MD 21740

The author assumes full responsibility for the accuracy of all
facts and quotations as cited in this book.

This book was
Edited by Jeannette R. Johnson
Copyedited by James Cavil
Electronic makeup by Shirley M. Bolivar
Cover designed by Edgerton•Bond Image Design/Mark Bond
Typeset: Veljovic Book 11/15

PRINTED IN U.S.A.

04 03 02 01 00   5 4 3 2 1

R&H Cataloging Service
Swanson, Gary B
    The moose, the goose, and the kingdom of God.
        1. Teenagers—Prayer book and devotions—English.
2. Religious life. I. Title.

ISBN 0-8280-1515-5

Contents

Works

"Truly, no ransom avails for one's life, there is no price one can give to God for it. For the ransom of life is costly, and can never suffice" (Ps. 49:7, 8, NRSV).

Spotty Success?

Sometimes spending a whole afternoon in a banyan tree can get to you. That's how it was for Lawrence. "A leopard's life is always the same thing," he fumed. "Day in and day out, a never-ending pursuit of something to eat. There must be something more to life than this," he grumbled to himself. "There has to be more than eating and sleeping."

Action under that particular banyan tree that day was pretty slow. The hot afternoon hours droned on like the dull screech of a cicada. And Lawrence had more time than usual to think. As he lay there, licking the soft pads of his forepaws, he looked for a few moments at the spots on his leg. Small black swirls they were, surrounded by brown-orange, and the more Lawrence thought about it, the more convinced he became that if he were going to make a change in his life, the first thing he'd have to do was to get rid of the spots—to change his appearance entirely.

Of course, this was a ridiculous idea. The notion that a full-grown leopard would have the ability—much less the desire—to change its spots was pretty radical. A leopard without its spotted coat was a pretty staggering concept.

"Yeah, right!" his friends snorted when they first heard of the idea. "Even if you could get rid of your spots, how would you hunt? Whether you noticed it or not, the spots on your back are perfect camouflage. If you were all one solid color in this environment, you'd be as obvious and as endangered as a block of ice! You'd starve in a week."

Lawrence didn't argue, but he'd made up his mind. Although he was sorry his friends didn't understand, he felt that he had made the right decision.

Then he happened upon Simon, a sinister serpent who was basking, half asleep, in the late-afternoon sun, too utterly satisfied to move. He had just finished off some poor animal that was now little more than a huge lump in his otherwise slender body. Lawrence and Simon had often talked together as they lay in wait along the same path to the water hole.

In passing, Lawrence mentioned his bold idea of making a change in his life, and it struck a glint of unusual interest in Simon's sleepy eyes. "You mean," he hissed, "you want to give up your spots *entirely?*"

Lawrence nodded.

"How, exactly, do you intend to go about doing that?" Simon asked. "It's an ennobling concept, of course," he said with oily ease, "but when it comes right down to it, Lawrence, what you're trying to do is impossible, you know—completely unnatural. You have no more control over the color and design of your coat than I do over my lack of legs. If I could have sprouted legs just because I'd decided to, don't you think I'd have done it long ago? It's no fun spending your entire life flat on your belly."

The conversation with Simon smothered Lawrence in a depression that nearly killed him. He took the rest of the week off from hunting and subsisted solely on water. What really bothered him was that Simon seemed to be so completely correct. There wasn't a thing he could do to change his spots. He didn't even know where to begin.

But at the end of the week his spirit seemed to rally a bit, and the germ of an idea was beginning to sprout in his brain. Maybe something could be done if he began slowly and didn't try to make too dramatic a change in his appearance all at once. First, he began by lying out in the direct sunlight at the hottest part of the day, thinking this would fade his spots a little. And, after several days of that, he glanced at his reflection in the water hole. Could he believe what he was seeing? Sure enough, his coat seemed to be lighter. Not anything so dramatic, of course, that he could be absolutely sure, but as he looked at himself he decided that he had indeed begun to make a change.

So when he ran into Simon again, he was just a little smug. He rippled the muscles under his coat and asked, "Notice anything different about me?"

Simon looked him over completely. "You've lost a little weight?" he guessed.

"No, that's not it," Lawrence growled. "Can't you see that my spots are lighter? I'm changing my coat."

Simon's eyes looked hazy at first, but then sharpened into venomous focus, and his mouth half opened in a high, sibilant laugh. "You mean you're still trying to change your spots?"

"Yes," Lawrence said.

"Well, I'm sorry as I can be, my friend, but you look exactly the same to me as when I saw you last. As a leopard, there doesn't seem to be a thing you can do to achieve a spotless reputation."

↻ If Lawrence's efforts "can never suffice" (Ps. 49:8, NRSV), what is the answer to his wish to change?

↻ What kinds of human behavior are equivalent to the spots that Lawrence wishes to change? Be specific.

↻ The next time you do a load of laundry, observe for a few minutes the way in which water and detergent swirl around and through the wash. Think about the inability of the soiled laundry to cleanse itself.

"God has done what the law, weakened by the flesh, could not do: by sending his own Son in the likeness of sinful flesh, and to deal with sin, he condemned sin in the flesh" (Rom. 8:3, NRSV).

Canoe

Once there was a man
who paddled his canoe
against the current
with great, sweeping strokes.
The muscles of his arms and shoulders
rippled like the twisting eddies,
curled and swirling round his oar blade
as he pulled it
through the water.
"There's a man," we said,
"who knows where he's going—
solid worker, heroic effort!"
But when we looked at the shore,
he was losing ground
just like the rest of us.
There's only one boatman
who ever made it on this river.

↪ How does Romans 8:3 relate to the man in the canoe?

↪ What is the proper place, if any, for works in the life of a Christian?

↪ Draw your own illustration of "Spotty Success?" or "Canoe."

Day 3

"I can do all things through Christ who strengthens me" (Phil. 4:13, NKJV).

Making a List and Checking It Twice

If ever there was a self-made man, it was Benjamin Franklin. Born into a poor home and a huge family, Franklin was soon apprenticed to become a printer. But from these humble beginnings he became one of the most prominent leaders in America's search for independence.

A list of his accomplishments reads like a small encyclopedia. He is credited with the invention of bifocals and the Franklin stove. He experimented in many fields of science. He was a prolific writer, and he carried out an active and effective career in diplomacy.

In one chapter of his autobiography Franklin describes his systematic attempt at self-improvement. Reasoning that he could improve his character by concentrating on specific traits, he outlined 13 areas of his life that he wished to improve. Going to work on one trait after another, he seemed to make some progress, but eventually gave up the process.

One of the reasons that Franklin never fully realized his goal of complete self-improvement was that he never recognized God's role in such an undertaking. He felt that he ought to be able to do all these things through human grit and determination. He was thinking *I can do all things* rather than *I can do all things through Christ*. Big difference!

In *Mere Christianity* C. S. Lewis explains it like this: "The Christian . . . does not think God will love us because we are good, but that God will make us good because He loves us; just as the roof of a greenhouse does not attract the sun because it is bright, but becomes bright because the sun shines on it."

↪ If Jesus is the "big difference," how do you account for changes that people make in their lives without His help?

↪ How would you answer a friend who claims that Christianity is just a crutch for weaklings?

↪ Meditate on Philippians 4:13. Think about what "all things" means to you personally.

Day 4

"By grace you have been saved through faith, and this is not your own doing; it is the gift of God—not the result of works, so that no one may boast" (Eph. 2:8, 9, NRSV).

Andrew

Two fishermen worked side by side.
Sorting through their morning catch,
they tossed the gleaming fishes
into three slippery piles.
For Andrew, yesterday's events
had been something
he would not soon forget.
    "It isn't as though
there was no food," he said.
"Among five thousand souls

will always be a certain few
who have provided for themselves.
Not all here follow Him around
like witless sheep.

"There was among them
many kinds of food—
here a basket of figs,
there a cheese or two—
or goat milk in a skin.
All was quickly covered
with a tunic or a robe,
or simply held behind one's back.

"The child's loaves were not the only
in so large a multitude."

Andrew straightened up
and stretched his aching back.
"To share one's food would,
to him with no imagination,
have been to surely go without.
They thought but did not say it:
let those who have been careless
fend for themselves.
Had He Himself not told the story
of the wise and foolish maidens?
And if someone deserves to go without,
surely it should be
the one who has not planned ahead.
So thought I;
so thought also the five thousand,

looking all around them
for someone else to solve their problem,
as though in days like these
we could expect again the manna.

    "The lesson isn't in the sharing,
but in the idea
that somehow He can provide.
We've seen Him multiply
the fishes in our nets before.
In that—as in almost all truth—
'a little child shall lead them.'
It's all part of what He meant
when He said we should be like children—
trusting *and* imaginative.
Giving to God isn't sharing at all
if you know He can give it back,
or return something far better.

    "Our Father Abraham taught us that
in the lesson of Moriah.
Sometimes I think the children
understand those old stories
better than we do."

    He held up one sorry fish—
stunted and deformed—
unsure of what to do with it.
"It all just makes you see
that He can make of us
more than we truly are—
that He can multiply the gifts

we bring to Him

as surely as He did

the child's humble loaves and fish."

↪ Andrew was a mere fisherman. Why is pride a problem even for those who, from a worldly viewpoint, come from lowly backgrounds?

↪ What do you consider to be the most important point in the report of Jesus' feeding of the five thousand?

↪ Pray that God will open your eyes to the miracles that are affecting your own life.

Day 5

"I do not understand what I do. For what I want to do I do not do, but what I hate I do" (Rom. 7:15, NIV).

Your Own Worst Enemy

The survival of China's giant panda has captured the imagination of millions of people around the world. When a panda was born at the Tokyo Zoo in 1986, 200,000 people a day phoned Dial-a-Panda just to hear a recording of the cub's squeal. The courtship of Washington National Zoo's Hsing Hsing and Ling Ling was reported daily in the press as though it were a soap opera. The San Diego Zoo sold a million panda T-shirts during the year it exhibited a pair of pandas.

At least part of the appeal of these animals is that they just look cute. Yet the world doesn't seem to be able to do what it takes to keep the panda from extinction. There are only about 1,000 left in the wild and 100 in captivity. And researchers point out that part of the problem is with the pandas themselves.

For one thing, at birth the young weigh only four ounces; they are blind and helpless. A mother panda delivers twins about 60 percent of the time, but she seldom attempts to keep the second one alive unless the first is stillborn.

Even their digestive tracts aren't right. They have the anatomy of a carnivore, but they live on a herbivore diet. Compared to a sheep, whose intestines are 25 times the length of its body, the panda's is only six times the length of its body. It has to eat 20 to 40 pounds of bamboo a day just to keep from starving to death.

So in some ways the panda isn't helping itself. It has to battle its own nature. And that is the way it is for Christians. We are born with a sinful nature that, in ourselves, we can do nothing about. In fact, we too often do exactly the opposite of what we want to do and what we know is right. Christ's righteousness alone can save us from extinction.

↻ In what ways has sin made humankind an endangered species?

↻ What behaviors in your life are self-destructive?

↻ Think about various campaigns to save endangered species. Compare their approaches and techniques with God's campaign to save humankind.

Day 6

"You who want to be justified by the law have cut yourselves off from Christ; you have fallen away from grace" (Gal. 5:4, NRSV).

Satire

What a sick joke

to take a hapless Prisoner

and, mocking His own words,

"Thou sayest,"

wrap Him in a purple robe

and force a crown of thorns

into His temple.

But what a grander joke—

the ultimate satire—

on those who in their self-importance

have presumed to wear

a crown and purple robe.

↪ Why was the crown of thorns an especially cruel joke?

↪ How do you respond to referring to Jesus' sacrifice as "the ultimate satire"? Explain your answer.

↪ As you watch a sunset, think of the night that Jesus died in your place.

Day 7

"[God] saved us and called us with a holy calling, not according to our works but according to his own purpose and grace. This grace was given to us in Christ Jesus before the ages began" (2 Tim. 1:9, NRSV).

Making It Personal

Try some of the following activities as you complete this week's consideration of the subject of works:

↪ Read the chapter "The Sermon on the Mount" in *The Desire of Ages.*

↪ List three people to whom you can demonstrate grace within the next few days through some act of undeserved kindness.

Look for opportunities to follow through on this list.

↻ After reviewing "Spotty Success?" write a parable of your own that communicates the futility of trying to change oneself without God's help.

↻ Find a way to demonstrate God's grace to you by helping in a voluntary organization in your community.

↻ Walk along the curb of a city block as you think about the idea of balance. Consider whether this experience of balance fairly represents the relationship between faith and works.

Jesus Christ

"I lay a stone in Zion, a tested stone, a precious cornerstone for a sure foundation; the one who trusts will never be dismayed" (Isa. 28:16, NIV).

A Bird on the Wing . . .

After countless generations of painstaking focus on detail, the chickadees finally had their tree in shape. They had it together! They had anticipated every possible contingency, and the Chickadee Tree stood as a perfectly symmetrical symbol of what could be accomplished if you demanded complete devotion to two guiding principles: technicality and uniformity. In fact, from these two seemingly self-evident principles, the chickadees had coined a name for their way of life: *techniformity*.

How to find a mate, conduct a business, care for your children, observe the holidays, prepare and eat the appropriate foods—everything was covered in the traditions that were passed down from the venerable Elders of the Graying Feathers, who inhabited the upper branches. They had spent whole lifetimes studying techniformity.

This august body traced its spiritual lineage back to the very first chickadee to come to this tree. Led by a quiet conviction that he had been called upon to leave his home tree many mountain ranges away and establish a whole new way of life, he had brought his small saucy family to this very site.

By now, countless generations later, the Elders of the Graying Feathers had developed a completely self-contained community. They didn't need anyone else in the surrounding forest. They had all their chickadees in a row. At least they thought they did, until a youngster named Chicklet quietly began to call into question just about every aspect of techniformity. And he was breaking laws left and right.

It was commonly known that Chicklet was the offspring of questionable parentage in one of the poorest nests on the very lowest branch of the tree. In the estimation of the Elders of the Graying Feathers, this in itself was a comment on his credibility. He was considered *dead last* in the pecking order. Who, after all, was going to take seriously anything this upstart said?

So although the Elders blithely tried for a time to ignore Chicklet and the small brood of ruffians and malcontents who had gathered around him, it just seemed that he kept turning up at the most inopportune moments and embarrassing them in front of the entire population of the Chickadee Tree. Well, if you're a member of the Elders of the Graying Feathers, you can't have someone repeatedly making a fool of you without losing the confidence of those in the lower branches! That is one of the long-established tenets of techniformity—of any system, for that matter.

What to do with this Chicklet?

You never heard such fussing and chattering and scolding—as only a treeful of chickadees can do—as they discussed the problem. Normally the Elders would have sought to settle the whole issue themselves, but Chicklet had gathered a small flock of his own, and they thought it would be politically expedient to involve the entire tree in solving the problem. Otherwise, they would be open to too much criticism, and Chicklet's growing popularity had already undermined their authority to an alarming degree.

Some had the courage to propose that they should simply

allow Chicklet's movement to run its course. If it had any value, they reasoned, then there would be no stopping it anyway. If it did not, then it would die a natural death, as had many other such uprisings throughout the long and revered history of the Chickadee Tree.

For others, this argument was far too laissez-faire. The only answer for them was banishment—the cruelest, most frightening kind of punishment that they could think of. For chickadees, normally a very gregarious species, banishment was brutal, final, eternal. It meant that the outcast would be forced to take wing and leave the Chickadee Tree forever, never to return. It meant that he would nevermore even be considered a member of the species. It meant nonexistence.

The Elders of the Graying Feathers skillfully manipulated the controversy so that those in the lower branches concluded that banishment was the only answer. Chicklet had brought to them the possibility of freedom from grinding techniformity, yet, ironically, the very chickadees who would have had most to benefit from this freedom actually threw their lot in with the Elders and demanded his banishment.

So Chicklet was forced to take wing and leave the Chickadee Tree. To the small clutch of followers he had left behind, there was a great deal of confusion and disillusionment. Had they flocked together with a bird of the wrong feather after all? What did it all mean?

Then, a short time later, while they were discussing these questions on one of the smaller, lower branches, Chicklet appeared right in the middle of them, seemingly out of nowhere. He perched on the limb with them as though nothing had happened.

This was unheard of. No one had ever returned from banishment.

Chicklet's reappearance changed everything. His flock soon realized that they weren't living in the true Chickadee Tree anymore. Over the generations it had changed, gradually and imperceptibly, into a techniform tree. And it had altered what it meant to be a chickadee. The *real* Chickadee Tree was now somewhere else, and Chicklet had returned to show them the way.

↻ In your opinion, what was Chicklet's most important accomplishment? Explain your answer.

↻ When, if ever, is it appropriate to defend the status quo?

↻ Explore the Internet for several Web sites that seek to present Jesus Christ to the world. Analyze two or three of these Web sites as to how they differ in their representation of Jesus.

Day 2

"I decided to know nothing among you except Jesus Christ, and him crucified" (1 Cor. 2:2, NRSV).

Secret Mission

The two had picked their way
across the noisy marketplace,
the question always whispering
from the darkest corners of their minds:
How will we know?
The animal looked to them
so much like any other—
so ordinary—
that they glanced at one another,
a little hesitant,
like two self-conscious boys
unsure, at last,
of what they were supposed to do.

In all these times

there had come to them

that moment to face,

to peer across the chasm of doubt—

the look before the leap.

But then at last

they recalled again

that He had sent them on such

missions of nonsense before,

so they repeated the password:

"The Lord has need of it . . ."

↻ Explain in your own words what is meant by the expression "missions of nonsense."

↻ In what way could it be said that it is a mission of nonsense to "know nothing . . . except Jesus Christ"?

↻ List five "missions of nonsense" in the Old Testament.

Day 3

"The Lord is my . . . salvation" (Ps. 27:1, NIV).

When the Chocolate Is Melting

Back in 1912 Clarence Crane's business had reached a critical turning point. As a chocolate maker he did very well from October through May. In the summer months, however, his business was literally melting away. Candy store owners wouldn't order his chocolate candy in June through September. Crane had to do something to stay in business, so he decided to produce hard candy mints as a summer line.

Because his chocolate-making machinery couldn't also produce hard candy, however, Crane went to a pill manufacturer. Everyone at the time thought of mint candy as shaped like tiny pillows: pinched around the edges and plump in the middle. Just to be unique, Crane had his mints made round, with a hole in the middle—just the size of a pill. "They look like little lifesavers," someone commented, and the candy industry will never be the same. The idea was a lifesaver for Crane's business too.

Jesus is our lifesaver. He's sweet. He's unique. He's just what is needed to solve our problems. He is our salvation when the chocolate is melting.

↪ What is the spiritual equivalent of the expression "when the chocolate is melting"?

↪ Think of at least three other modern-day concepts that could symbolize the importance of Jesus' ministry to the world.

↪ Purchase a roll of Lifesavers and place them in a location where they will remind you periodically of Jesus as your personal lifesaver.

Day 4

"[John the Baptist] saw Jesus coming toward him and declared, 'Here is the Lamb of God who takes away the sin of the world!'" (John 1:29, NRSV).

Simon the Cyrene

"The jeers and screams
of the crowd echoed
along the walls of the side streets,
and I went to see

what the commotion was about.
I had nothing better to do."

Simon's wife brought him some bread
and, laying it on the table before him,
sat down to listen.

"Did you see the Temple?"
she asked.

But he forged on
as though he had not heard her question.
"The Roman soldiers
were taking a man out of the city
to crucify him.
I've never seen a crowd like that one:
they would have torn him apart
if it hadn't been for the soldiers."

"Are you going to tell me
about Jerusalem," she pouted,
"or about the execution
of some miserable criminal?"

He smiled and shook his head.
"It is a city like any other—
good and bad,
rich and poor,
clean and dirty.

"The Temple? Yes, it is beautiful—
so white and gleaming.
It seems to glow long after sundown.
But nothing in all that magnificent city
affected me the way

his face did;
I'll never forget it."

"Whose face?"

"The man they crucified.
He stumbled as he passed—
he was exhausted.
One of the soldiers
tapped me on the shoulder with his sword.
'Take it up!' he ordered.
So I carried the cross to the hill."

She was aghast.
"You carried the cross
of a common criminal?
How could you get involved
in such a thing?"

"He was innocent;
I don't know why
the others couldn't see it."

He shrugged.
"Maybe they just didn't want to."

↪ Do you think that the average person should have been able to recognize Jesus as the Messiah simply by His appearance? Explain your answer.

↪ If you had lived in the time of Jesus' ministry on this earth, what would have been the most telling evidence to you personally that He was the Messiah?

↪ List three specific things you can do in the next 24 hours that would help others to see Jesus in you.

Day 5

"Blessed are you when people insult you, persecute you and falsely say all kinds of evil against you because of me" (Matt. 5:11, NIV).

Dingbat Christianity

"Edith, you're a dingbat!" This was the ultimate put-down for the hit television series *All in the Family*. The show was so successful, in fact, that the favorite chair of the bigot Archie Bunker is now on display at the Smithsonian Institute in Washington, D.C.

Almost every week Archie Bunker made fun of his wife Edith's simple approach to life. Throughout the series Edith was depicted as the naive yet endearing character who held the family together in her own unique way.

The producer of the show, Norman Lear, once made the curious statement that the character of Edith Bunker was based on Jesus Christ. "We always thought Edith would react to things exactly the way Jesus would," Lear told a newspaper reporter. "She's somebody who swallowed the Sermon on the Mount and lived it. And that was always our guideline for Edith."

At first blush Edith Bunker may seem an unexpected example of Christian living, but the idea does make sense in some ways. In the eyes of the world a Christian who has "swallowed the Sermon on the Mount and lived it" would indeed be considered a dingbat. Such people would be viewed as so out of step with the rest of the world that their quality of mind would be in question. They would certainly be insulted by those who do not understand the great promises of the Sermon on the Mount.

In the decades right after Jesus' death the name Christian had at first very negative connotations, but the followers of Jesus took it up with increasing reverence. Although the name "dingbat" will surely never attain such status in our society, one could do worse than to be called dingbat by the world.

- Does Matthew 5:11 mean that a Christian will always be an unpopular figure? Explain your answer.

- Explain why you agree or disagree that the popular media are not an appropriate source for a search for Jesus.

- List the names of several television shows with which you are familiar. Think about which character among these shows is most Christlike.

Day 6

"He took up our infirmities and carried our sorrows, yet we considered him stricken by God, smitten by him, and afflicted. But he was pierced for our transgressions, he was crushed for our iniquities; the punishment that brought us peace was upon him, and by his wounds we are healed" (Isa. 53:4, 5, NIV).

Dress Code

If you saw Jesus walking
     past your house this morning,
          what would He be wearing?
Botany 500,
     wing-tip shoes,
     and power ties?
Something sensible from Sears,
     color-coded mix-'n'-match,
          made to "wear like iron"?
Boston Red Sox baseball cap,
     red plaid flannel shirt,
     woolen socks and Levis
          whitening at the knees?

Army-surplus combat jacket,
soleless wing-tip shoes
(once or twice removed)
and no socks at all?
Would He be wearing something that—
if we lynched Him again—
the police would raffle off?
What kind of wardrobe
does He need
to fit into your neighborhood?

↪ To what extent must Jesus be culturally compatible for people to accept Him?

↪ To what extent does appearance affect the way in which you respond to people?

↪ By freehand or computer, create a small poster on which you represent your favorite saying of Jesus. Post it somewhere in your home and make copies available to friends who would like them.

Day 7

"The Word became flesh and made his dwelling among us. We have seen his glory, the glory of the One and Only, who came from the Father, full of grace and truth" (John 1:14, NIV).

Making It Personal

Try some of the following activities as you complete this week's consideration of the subject of Jesus Christ:

↻ Phone five members of your home church and ask each the

question: If you had lived in the time of Jesus' ministry on this earth, what would have been the most telling evidence to you personally that He was the Messiah? After you have elicited this information, share and discuss your findings with a friend.

↻ Design an imaginary postage stamp that would express in a single image what Jesus Christ's ministry means to humanity.

↻ From the Internet, download a genealogical program into which you can enter the information from Jesus' family tree as it is outlined in Matthew 1. Think about the importance of Jesus' family tree as it pertains to His claim to be the Messiah.

↻ Look through some books of classic art in which Jesus is depicted. Think about the feelings that these works of art evoke in you about the character of Jesus.

↻ Read the chapters "'God With Us'" and "Unto You a Saviour" in *The Desire of Ages*.

Conversion

"All the ways of the Lord are loving and faithful for those who keep the demands of his covenant" (Ps. 25:10, NIV).

Overcoming Overbite

Once there was a man who hung out his shingle and opened an office of spiritual orthodontia. This was actually a pretty revolutionary idea in those days because it was offering a whole new approach to straightening out one's life. *Orthodontia* and *orthodox* were two terms that—at that time—were not considered to have derived from the same root word. Till then, people were experimenting with a wide variety of do-it-yourself techniques and approaches, all of them leading to some of the most grotesque and twisted lives you can imagine.

"Let's see, now," the spiritual orthodontist would say to one of his new patients who had come into his office for a personal consultation. "The first thing we'll have to do is extract a couple cherished habits in your life to make room for other behaviors that are more positive. Then we'll move some of these less developed practices forward—little by little—to fill in the gaps that you have. Before you know it, you'll have a life as straight as an arrow that Moses or Joseph or Daniel would have been proud of!"

Because of the unorthodox nature of his radical claims, the orthodontist's business was less than brisk at first, as one might expect. Most new ideas go through a "learning curve," during which the general public is suspicious at best and cynical at worst. And this, of course, does not include the outright reaction of hostility from those who considered themselves to be authorities in the time-honored, well-established field of life straightening. The experts convened upper-echelon think tanks and consensus conferences and announced to the press scathing references to the orthodontist's process as being nothing more than another snake-oil approach that the uneducated and superstitious had given up eons before. To tell the truth, this was an ironic reaction because, when it came right down to it, snake oil was the very essence of all other conventional treatments of the day.

But despite the negative reaction of the establishment, the orthodontist was eager to make the world aware of his amazing new service. He didn't want to have to rely merely on word of mouth, so to speak. So, with uncommon missionary zeal, he began to advertise in all the most highly circulated life-straightening media of the day.

This is how his claims read:

"Thanks to an amazingly simple breakthrough that has been overlooked for centuries, you can have a life as straight as those of the patriarchs. Using the principles of orthodontia applied in the past only for teeth, the spiritual orthodontist can fit you with a set of braces that will straighten your life out like the road to Damascus."

To be fair, it must be pointed out here that—like most language of marketing—this was never meant to be interpreted literally because, of course, the road to Damascus is anything but geographically straight. It was a way of claiming that someone could have his or her life straightened the way Paul's life was going to be straightened *on* the road to Damascus, and this, of course, hadn't actually occurred yet. The spiritual orthodontist had a sometimes disturbingly unscientific way of anticipating events that left the stubborn and the uninformed a little confused about literal time and place.

"For a smile that will last an *eternity,*" the marketing claims went on to say, "see the spiritual orthodontist today!"

Well, who could turn away from such an opportunity as this? The marketing campaign had an immediate and galvanizing impact. The lights on the telephone extensions in the orthodontist's office lit up like a Christmas tree. There were all kinds of questions for his receptionists to answer, most of them completely irrelevant to the real issue, that is, the actual need for straightening out one's life. So the receptionists had to do their best to answer silly questions such as "Does the process hurt?" "Can I afford it?" "What will it cost me?" "Will it be covered by my insurance?" "Are there any age limitations?" "Can I wait a year or two and have it done later?"

The greatest and most perplexing problem, however, was that way down deep in the hearts of so many consumers, people simply refused to believe that they needed spiritual orthodontia at all. And, amazingly, many were just plain unwilling to give up the care and treatment of their lives to the spiritual orthodontist. They thought they could straighten themselves out, could tinker with this problem or slightly adjust that and, little by little, some day they would have things all lined up in a neat, orderly row. The so-called experts and authorities would look in the mirror in the morning, smile confidently to themselves, and completely overlook the ghastliness of their own overbites.

⟳ How is conversion like "spiritual orthodontia"? How is it different?

⟳ What is the spiritual equivalent of each of the following questions: "Does the process hurt?" "Can I afford it?" "What will it cost me?" "Will it be covered by my insurance?" "Are there any age limitations?" "Can I wait a year or two and have it done later?"

↪ In prayer, invite Jesus to become your spiritual orthodontist. Ask Him to communicate to you the ways in which your life needs straightening.

"You were washed, you were sanctified, you were justified in the name of the Lord Jesus Christ and by the Spirit of our God" (1 Cor. 6:11, NIV).

Desert Baker

With just a word
  on any day of forty
He could have turned
  the desert stones to bread.
He could have made
  the wilderness
    a bakery shop—
    the fragrance of it
      wafting a half mile away:
        dill or rye or poppy seed,
        cinnamon or caraway.
He chose instead
  to feed and not be fed,
    the simplest of recipes—
      without so much as leaven—
He is both word and bread.

↪ What implications does the following quotation suggest to you:

"He is both word and bread"?

↻ What role does Jesus play in conversion? Be specific.

↻ Read through a recipe for the baking of bread. Think about the spiritual applications of both the ingredients and the process.

Day 3

"There is a way that seems right to a person, but its end is the way to death" (Prov. 14:12, NRSV).

Amazing Pathfinders

For decades Yale University professor Talbot Waterman studied the ways that animals find their way in the world. "At times," he says, "animal pathfinding requires skills that seem to verge on clairvoyance, primarily because animals use different or more acute senses than those humans use."

Spiders, for instance, have sensors near their leg joints that help them keep track of where they've been. The inner ears of gerbils help them remember every twist and turn they have taken in the dark, underground passages where they live. Fiddler crabs can judge direction by the position of the sun—even on cloudy days—because the corneas of their compound eyes have thousands of facets, each of which is sensitive to the angle of polarized light. Milkweed bugs seem to have an inherited memory for direction. The migration of this insect takes two or three generations to complete, but they always end up at the same place at the same time.

Humankind was created with a spiritual sense of direction, but unfortunately we have elected to go our own way. Little by little, by giving in to one temptation after another, we have become so lost that we no longer know right from wrong. We may be doing something that seems right, but we're on a path that "is the way to death."

That's why it is so important to use the spiritual sensors that we were created with—to keep our eyes on Jesus. In that way we will be able to end up in the right place at the right time.

☞ Select one of the following examples and explore its spiritual interpretation: a spider's leg-joint sensors; a gerbil's inner ear; a fiddler crab's cornea; a milkweed bug's inherited memory.

☞ In everyday terms, how can we know whether a chosen path "is the way to death"?

☞ Think of two other examples from nature that would illustrate how a Christian should stay on the path to salvation.

Day 4

"Create in me a pure heart, O God, and renew a steadfast spirit within me" (Ps. 51:10, NIV).

Nicodemus

He sat down next to Joseph
near the cavernous hole
at midmorning
to sort out what had happened.
A hasty look around—
the stone rolled back,
the tomb a vacuum,
the bands of cloth
they'd wrapped him in
folded neatly and left behind.
"One of the first things
that attracted me to Him,"

Nicodemus said,
"was His penchant for paradox.
His ideas ran counter—
completely the opposite—
to everything we've been taught.
  "'He who is first shall be last!'
There's a revolutionary idea for you—
something a Zealot would gulp down
like a hungry dog.
(But even the Zealots, I would guess,
misunderstood His message.)
  "A year ago, or more,
I went to see Him one night—
I wish now I'd had the courage
to go to Him in the daylight,
but He didn't act
as though it made any difference—
and I asked Him
questions about Himself
that had been puzzling me."
  Joseph added nothing,
idly plucking at the brittle grass
that grew all over the hillside.
  "I went to see Him,"
Nicodemus repeated,
"and He told me,
'You must be born again.'
Now, doesn't that sound
just like Him?

I've been pondering

that statement ever since.

But now, finally this morning—

now that we know

He's alive again—

I'm beginning to make

a little sense of it.

What is His resurrection

but a new birth for us?"

↻ What saying of Jesus has been most puzzling to you?

↻ In practical terms, how can we know what changes God expects of us? Be specific.

↻ Some computer software manuals use the words *convert* and *conversion* to describe changes from one form to another. Explore a couple of these usages to see what they add to your understanding of spiritual conversion.

Day 5

"By faith Moses, when he was come to years, refused to be called the son of Pharaoh's daughter; choosing rather to suffer affliction with the people of God, than to enjoy the pleasures of sin for a season" (Heb. 11:24, 25).

Making Waves

An old sailing tradition dictates that if fog closes in on a harbor and prevents small-boat sailors from seeing or hearing the buoy to find their way, the sailors immediately begin to turn their little craft in small circles. Then they stop and listen intently. The waves resulting from this technique begin to rock the buoy and make the bell clang. Then the sailors can continue on their way.

By making waves, sailors can find their way back to the safety of the harbor. But sailing around in tight circles can be dangerous. They have to take a calculated risk to achieve their goal.

It isn't possible to improve yourself in this life without facing some risk. Learning what risks to take is an important stepping-stone to achievement. But sometimes we take risks seemingly for the enjoyment of it.

When Moses forsook the tremendous opportunities he had in Pharaoh's court and decided to side with his countrymen, he was taking a great risk. From the human standpoint, he was giving up wealth, fame, power, and education.

But Moses' faith was strong enough that he knew this was what God wanted him to do. In order to find his way through the fog at that time in his life, he had to make waves. And because of his choice to take these risks, God guided him through the enticements of one of the world's greatest civilizations to a safety and security that lasts forever.

↻ To what extent is risk involved in becoming a Christian?

↻ How would you encourage someone whose fear of risk-taking is preventing him or her from accepting Christ? Be practical and specific.

↻ Interview three recent converts from your home church. Ask them to explain their thought processes as they decided to accept Jesus as their personal Saviour.

Day 6

"The fear of the Lord is a fountain of life, so that one may avoid the snares of death" (Prov. 14:27, NRSV).

My Father Says . . .

When I was 9,
> my father likened me to a snowflake,
>> each one unique.

But I could never take
> much comfort being like a snowflake.

When it snows,
> the ground is white;
>> as far as you can see—
> one snowflake's contribution
>> doesn't cut much ice.

And it takes a microscope
> to see the difference anyway.

Who would ever take the time
> to look so close at me?

Then the snowflakes melt away
> in springtime when all else
>> is ready to begin.

No thanks!
I think I'd rather be
> like all the rest

if, by doing that,
> I could somehow survive the melt—
>> if that could be arranged.

If snowflakes were forever, now,
> I'd settle for uniqueness too.

Then that would count for something.
My father smiled and said

that snowflakes *do* survive

by being changed

"in the twinkling of an eye"—

so much of what my father said

makes me want to laugh and cry.

↪ State in a single sentence the meaning of the poem "My Father Says . . ." to you personally.

↪ Why does spiritual truth sometimes make someone "want to laugh and cry"?

↪ Select one of the scriptural passages in this week's readings and meditate on what it means to your personally. Pray that God will give you one new fresh insight into the plan for your life.

Day 7

"In the way of righteousness there is life; along that path is immortality" (Prov. 12:28, NIV).

Making It Personal

Try some of the following activities as you complete this week's consideration of the subject of conversion:

↺ Some computer programs use *conversion* to designate a change from one format to another. Consider how this may or may not be analogous with conversion to Christianity.

↺ Read the chapter "'Like Unto Leaven'" in *Christ's Object Lessons*.

↺ On the Internet, explore some Web sites devoted to research on the human brain. Think about the role of the brain in one's conversion to Christianity. What is the role of intellect? of emotion? How can one know that his or her conversion is a safe balance between the two?

↺ Play a recording on cassette or CD and/or perform vocally or instrumentally the hymn "I Surrender All" (number 309 in *The Seventh-day Adventist Hymnal*). What do the words of this hymn suggest about the experience of conversion?

↺ Read a book about the Christian conversion of someone from another faith. Think about the risks and changes that the person faced as he or she gave up one way of life for another. Consider how these issues may be instructive in your own life.

Temptation

"Do not enter the path of the wicked, and do not walk in the way of evildoers. Avoid it; do not go on it; turn away from it and pass on" (Prov. 4:14, 15, NRSV).

Honk if You're Flying South

Gus, a year-old gosling, knew only one thing for sure: that he had to keep flapping ever onward—always with his neck stretched out toward the south. It was a fine autumn, and he was headed for a warmer climate with his family and friends. Everything was right on schedule. But even at best, flying south was certainly no picnic at this time of year—scrounging around for food in barren cornfields; keeping out of range of the hunters' guns; sleeping on icy ponds.

One morning Gus chanced to overhear a couple 2-year-olds in his flock talking in hushed tones about something they called a hot spring. He was aware that they had made the trip south before, and they clearly knew their way around. They were experienced. Gus had never heard of a hot spring before, but it sounded to him as though it had to be just about the nicest thing he could imagine. So he mustered up the courage to ask very casually, "Hey, you guys know where I can find any hot springs around here?"

His question seemed to startle the 2-year-olds. "What do you know about hot springs?" one of them asked, with a quick look around him.

"Enough," Gus said, yawning elaborately. He already could tell that it must be pretty cool to know something about hot springs.

The 2-year-olds exchanged a quick glance and a knowing smile. "I think maybe we can put you in touch with something," one of them said. "Stay cool. We'll get back to you."

Toward the end of that day the V began to descend gently toward a silvery lake for the night. Gus flew the next-to-the-last position on the long side of the V, the traditional place for goslings. But anyone with feathers could tell that winter was right behind them, breathing down their necks, and Gus looked at the icy water below him with a shudder. *The last thing I need right now,* he thought, *is cold water. Why don't we just keep heading southward?*

Just as he was putting his flaps down, however, one of the 2-year-olds swept past him. "Follow us," he whispered. "There's a hot spring just the other side of that hill." For the merest fraction of a second Gus hesitated. To go away from the rest of the group was dangerous. That was well-established goose wisdom. But the thought of a hot spring! This was something he would have to experience for himself. He couldn't possibly pass up an opportunity like this. After all, the other two had been there before, and he'd be with them.

And it wasn't really very far away after all, just as the 2-year-olds had predicted. Steam rose invitingly from its surface. The three of them circled once around it, lowered their landing gear, and slipped with a sigh of satisfaction into the water. What a feeling! It was better by far than anything Gus could have imagined. It completely removed him from the cold, advancing winter. This was a different world!

After a while one of the 2-year-olds prepared to leave. "Come on," he said. We have to join the V at the lake before it gets too dark or we could miss takeoff in the morning."

"I think maybe you'd better go on without me for now," Gus

said. "I'm going to stay just a little longer. I've never felt this good before, and I don't want to leave." The others grinned at each other, shrugged, and rose from the steaming water.

As darkness closed around him, Gus fell comfortably asleep. In fact, he slept there through the entire night. When he woke the next morning, he was tired and lonely. Although the water was still deliciously warm, he knew the others would be leaving soon and felt the need to be joining them. He could hear the far-off honking of the geese as the V rose from the lake and began their day's journey. When he attempted to rise from the water, however, he felt as if his strength were gone. The hot spring had become a comfortable trap. But desperation sparked something deep inside him. With more effort than he knew he had, he rose from the water and went in search of the others.

As Gus took a place at the very end of the V, he now regretted he'd ever gone to the hot spring. It had felt good, no doubt about it. But it had left him drained. He knew he'd have a difficult time keeping up for the rest of the day. *Never again,* he said to himself. *This is one goose that isn't going to get cooked!*

↪ Note the four parts of the counsel in overcoming temptation listed in Proverbs 4:15. How are these four parts different from each other?

↪ Apply the four parts of Proverbs 4:15 to the parable "Honk if You're Flying South."

↪ Underline, highlight, or otherwise mark the scriptural references that appear at the beginning of each day's part of this week's readings. In your future Bible reading, watch for other counsel in overcoming temptation.

"No testing has overtaken you that is not common to everyone. God is faithful, and he will not let you be tested beyond your strength, but with the testing he will also provide the way out so that you may be able to endure it" (1 Cor. 10:13, NRSV).

Novitiate

The preacher called it
> "the watery grave,"
and then buried me
> in its liquid warmth.
I was 10,
> but I knew nothing then.
Sin was stealing Hershey Bars from Safeway
and lying about a window broken,
> and salvation was just the opposite.
But as the years' time-lapse petals unfold,
> sin branches out
> > like a crystal tree
> into intricate possibilities,
and looking at it would dazzle me
> if salvation weren't still so simple.

↪ "If salvation weren't still so simple." In this context, does the word *simple* mean "easy" or "uncomplicated" or something else? Explain your choice.

↪ State the three major points of 1 Corinthians 10:13 in your own words.

↪ For each of the three major points of 1 Corinthians 10:13, find an Old Testament story that would serve as an illustration.

Day 3

"Avoid every kind of evil" (1 Thess. 5:22, NIV).

Too Close for Comfort

Late in 1992 the dumbbell-shaped, four-mile-long asteroid Toutatis whisked by the earth so perilously close that it sent scientists scrambling for a way to prevent anything from slamming into us and destroying life as we know it. OK, so it missed us by 2.2 million miles! Considering the vastness of the cosmos, that's a hair's breadth. And astronomers say it's only a matter of time before some heavenly body bears down on earth. They've specifically counted more than 100 asteroids (and estimated another 2,000) traveling as fast as 135,000 mph that would have impact energies ranging from 100,000 to many millions of megatons and that pass through earth's orbit.

So what can we do about it? Researchers say that if an incoming asteroid is detected soon enough, we could dispatch a missile to explode near enough to it to deflect it out of its path and away from the earth. To hit it directly with an explosion could break it up into countless chunks that would still be dangerous to life on earth.

In such plans no one seems to be suggesting, "Hey, wouldn't it be exciting to watch it narrowly miss us? What a show that would be!" No, humankind is interested only in how much distance it can place between itself and a collision course with an asteroid.

Yet, oddly, we aren't always the same way with evil, which is every bit as dangerous. We think we can drift closer and closer to sin without being sucked into its gravitational pull. That's why Paul wrote to the Thessalonians, "Avoid every kind of evil." He knew that you can't make exceptions in the life-and-death struggle with temptation.

↪ If there is only one kind of sin (separation from God), what do you think Paul means by "every *kind* of evil"?

In everyday terms, how does one "avoid every kind of evil"? List some ways.

Phone a close friend and ask him or her to pray for you as you seek to overcome some specific temptation in your life.

"Put on the whole armor of God, so that you may be able to stand against the wiles of the devil" (Eph. 6:11, NRSV).

Mary Magdalene

She knew who it was
by the way he tapped on the door,
and for a moment she considered
leaving the door unanswered.
But then she also knew
she'd have to face him somewhere—
in the street or marketplace—
and though he never would
acknowledge her in public,
he'd corner her somewhere
and demand an explanation.
She knew that.

She threw back the bolt,
and he stole in
with a furtive look
up and down the street.

"What took you so long?"
he asked. "You know

I mustn't be seen
loitering around out there."

"I wasn't going
to let you in," she said.

"Oh, really?" he snorted.
"You thought to whet my appetite
by depriving me awhile?
Water tastes its sweetest
in the driest desert," he winked.
Her weak attempts at resolve
had always fanned his fire.

He reached for her;
she recoiled at his touch
and turned away.
"I cannot—will not—
let you in this house again.
I'm going to change my life—
or let the Master change it."

He flashed a knowing smile.
"So that's it!
You think that after all you've done—
all the times you've tried and failed—
you can be as good as anybody else!"

"It doesn't matter
what I've done before," she said.
"I finally realized that.
I can be new and clean."

His eyes began to smolder.
"You will be needing someone;

wait and see," he snarled.

"And when you do,

don't come looking for me!"

He stalked out

and slammed the door behind him.

"I won't," she murmured

to an empty room.

↻ What is meant by the "armor of God"? Be specific.

↻ Why is temptation more difficult to overcome when you've given in to it before?

↻ Draw an illustration of the "armor of God" as it would appear if it were the protective equipment of a baseball catcher or ice hockey goaltender.

Day 5

"We do this so that we may not be outwitted by Satan; for we are not ignorant of his designs" (2 Cor. 2:11, NRSV).

Our Defense Tactics

In his book *Arctic Dreams* Barry Lopez describes the craftiness of the polar bear. He says that this great hunter of the far north probably uses more strategies than any other predator in capturing and killing its prey.

The polar bear has developed such a wide arsenal of hunting techniques that it has become very proficient at killing ringed seals. It may take a half hour in the water to approach a resting seal on an ice floe, surfacing silently to see where it is and then submerging again. It may drift like a small harmless iceberg to within striking distance, then explode from the water so suddenly and ferociously that the seal has no time to react. When it is stalking a seal on the ice, it slithers along in the snow on its chest and forelegs. It will build small mounds of snow to hide behind while it waits at the edge of a seal's breathing hole in the ice. It will even surface in the seal's covered den and catch it sleeping there. Or it can smell the den buried under the snow and crash into it so quickly that the seal cannot escape.

It may seem that the ringed seal is completely helpless against its enemy. It does, however, have certain ways to protect itself. While it rests close to its breathing hole, it looks up for six or eight seconds every 20 to 30 seconds. At the slightest sound it slips quickly and silently into the water. Researchers have found that for all its cleverness, the polar bear is successful in killing ringed seals only about 20 percent of the time.

"Only those who try to resist temptation know how strong it is," says C. S. Lewis in *Mere Christianity*. "You find out the strength of a wind by trying to walk against it, not by lying down." Like ringed seals, a Christian must be aware of the crafty techniques of the enemy. In both cases this is a matter of survival!

↪ In what specific ways can we overcome ignorance of Satan's designs?

↪ Explain why you agree or disagree with the following statement: All sin begins with temptation.

↪ Think about a TV show you have seen in which a character is tempted to do something wrong. How did he or she respond to it?

"Can one walk on hot coals without scorching the feet?" (Prov. 6:28, NRSV).

True Blue

I've always thought that blue
        was the best color on the palette.
I like to leave it there—
        squeezed full and pure,
        glistening in an S-shaped curl
            right out of the tube.
But then something always seems
        to make me wonder
            if just a touch of yellow—
                just the slightest hint of yellow—
            might not make it bluer.
So with the needle point
        of my finest brush,
I touch a breath of yellow
        to the blue—no difference,
            at least as far as I can see.
Maybe one more dab,
        I tell myself,
            would give it just the right hue—
                quintessential blue.
It goes on like this
        until I'm lost somewhere in green—
            totally disoriented.

Then I reach again

for the tube of blue

and wonder why,

if I like blue so much,

I always mess it up.

↻ What connection do you see between Proverbs 6:28 and the poem "True Blue"?

↻ How do Proverbs 6:28 and the poem "True Blue" relate to the subject of temptation?

↻ For a week, carry some small blue object in your purse or pocket. Whenever you see it, think about the effect that temptation has had on your life and ask God's help in overcoming it.

Day 7

"Submit yourselves therefore to God. Resist the devil, and he will flee from you" (James 4:7, NRSV).

Making It Personal

Try some of the following activities as you complete this week's consideration of the subject of temptation:

↺ Watch a nature documentary on the subject of snakes. Afterward, think about why the snake was chosen as the medium through which to tempt Adam and Eve. What is the principle behind temptation that one can learn from such a choice?

↺ In a book or on the Internet, look up some quotations that pertain to the subject of temptation. Copy down two or three that are particularly meaningful to you.

- Write a poem in first person (like "Mary Magdalene"), in which Eve is looking back years after leaving Eden and commenting on her experience with the serpent.

- Read the chapters "The Temptation" and "The Victory" in *The Desire of Ages*.

- With several friends, form a prayer group that will meet regularly and pray for one another as you seek to overcome sin in your lives.

Faith

"Blessed is the man who makes the Lord his trust, who does not look to the proud, to those who turn aside to false gods" (Ps. 40:4, NIV).

Taking Leif of His Senses

Leif was a wiry little maple sapling whose oversized ambition was to grow into the strongest tree in the forest. He looked above him at the towering trees with their stout, spreading branches and said to himself with determination, *Just wait and see. Someday I'll be king of the whole forest!* It was a great aspiration for such a small and insignificant treelet. If the truth were told, he was a very thin, willowy little fellow, brashly pushing his way through the warm humus carpet laid down by his huge neighbors, the pines and poplars and cedars and oaks.

But although he loved the rich humus of the older trees, he always resented the fact that they thought they were smarter and more experienced than he was and that they always wanted to give him unasked-for advice. "Keep your leaves facing the sun," they seemed to enjoy reminding him, or "Drive your roots down as deep as you can into the rich soil." *It is positively irksome the way they're always preaching to me,* he fumed. *They never give a young tree credit for having any sap of his own!*

Leif especially disliked one piece of counsel that the whole forest repeated over and over. "Don't grow up in the shade of a larger tree," his neighbors intoned. "The nutrients in the soil will not support trees growing too close to each other." Some bookish box elder had come up with it something like a thousand years before, and no one even considered questioning its wisdom.

But for some reason Leif had decided to rebel on this very point. He was especially proud that he had taken root under the very shadow of a powerful giant black oak near the peak of a hill. His theory was that, sheltered as he was from the fearsome west wind, he could grow strong and untouched until the day when lightning would surely strike his huge neighbor. Then Leif would quickly rise from the shadows of his fallen protector and become king—it was just as easy as that.

And, as much as the older trees in the forest hated to acknowledge it, Leif was growing steadily. When the wind came up, his giant neighbor, groaning and twisting, caught the brunt of it. When hailstorms pelted the hillside, the black oak took the beating. When the heavy snows came, the giant's broad, strong trunk kept the snow off Leif's twiglike branches. It was a soft life, he thought—the only way to become a king.

Then one electrifying, blue-gray day when clouds were rumbling across the sky like a buffalo herd, the final phase of Leif's plan went into effect. This was the moment he'd been waiting for. Lightning pierced the sky like cannon shot and struck the giant at the very top, splitting it in two and sending it to the ground with a splintering, earthshaking crash. The magnificent oak lay there at the top of the hill, nothing more than a smoldering heap of its former self.

At long last, Leif thought in triumph, *I'm going to get my chance. This will show that old box elder that I know what I'm doing.* And as the clouds rolled away, the sky turned majestically blue and the sun came out and cast a golden glow all over the hilltop, spotlighting Leif as though God Himself were ordaining his coronation.

The other trees in the forest—the hickories and the birches

and the junipers—were suddenly very impressed. The whisperings through the leaves and needles for miles around could not seem to deny it: here was a revolutionary way to become somebody. New seedlings immediately sprouted at the very base of larger trees and began the expectant watch for their downfall.

But as the winter rolled around, the fallacy of Leif's plan began to make itself seen. Without his strong neighbor, he had to brave the elements without a developed defense of his own. Now he had to lean and twist in the wind on his own; now he had to withstand the pounding hailstorms; now his own undeveloped branches strained under merciless loads of snow. And because he had grown so close to the giant, Leif was simply unprepared for the responsibility thrust upon him so abruptly.

As the snows of winter slowly melted away and ran off in rivulets down the hill, Leif, his branches broken and twisted, lost his roothold and tottered pathetically to the ground. Instead of commanding the peak of the hill for centuries, as he had hoped, Leif lost his reign in little more than a season. The old-timers nodded their heads knowingly. With a pitying sigh sifting softly through their branches, the trees of the forest repeated the old adage passed from one generation to another: "Don't grow up in another tree's shadow."

↪ How does the parable "Taking Leif of His Senses" relate to the subject of faith?

↪ Does faith in God preclude self-reliance completely? Explain your answer.

↪ List five people—or groups of people—in whom you place your faith on a daily basis.

"Blessed are those whose strength is in you, who have set their hearts on pilgrimage" (Ps. 84:5, NIV).

The Magi's Star

Was the Magi's star

a matter of astronomy—

of telescopes and sextants

and light-years;

or of theology—

of faith and love and hope?

Or is there a difference?

Whether one or the other or both,

it truly was a heavenly body.

↪ In what respects is faith a pilgrimage?

↪ Are faith and science mutually exclusive? Explain your answer.

↪ Take some quiet time to listen to sounds going on around you. Think about which of these sounds enhance your faith in God.

"Rejoice and be glad, because great is your reward in heaven" (Matt. 5:12, NIV).

Step by Step

"Hard work, step by step, long hours." This is how Børge Ousland described his solo 64-day journey across Antarctica in 1997. Braving temperatures of as low as -69°F, the 34-year-old

Norwegian doggedly skied cross-country for 1,675 miles through an all-white world from the Berkner Island in the Weddell Sea to the Ross Sea. When the weather allowed, he was able to attach a sail to his waist to boost him along, which one day helped him to cover 140 miles. Otherwise, it was just one ski ahead of the other, hauling behind him a sled with 400 pounds of supplies.

Sometimes it's tempting to consider the pursuit of the Christian lifestyle, with its demands and expectations, to be as dull, pointless, and lonely as Ousland's trip across the Antarctic continent. At times like this it is encouraging to consider a few things: first, the strength to pursue such a course comes not from within but from a God who loves us; second, the quest that lies before us has already been conquered by Jesus, who faced every obstacle that could come our way; and, third, the goal of such an expedition is someday to become reunited with Him forever.

This does not suggest, of course, that the Christian life is easy. From the human viewpoint, it is still "hard work, step by step, long hours." George MacDonald says in *Donal Grant*, "Love and faith and obedience are sides of the same prism." But we should "rejoice and be glad, because great is [our] reward in heaven."

☛ Earlier in this book you read that "there doesn't seem to be a thing you can do to achieve a spotless reputation" (see page 9). How do you reconcile this statement with the idea that the Christian life is "hard work, step by step, long hours"?

☛ What kind of specific effort *is* expected of a Christian?

☛ Take a "tactile" field trip around your home. Collect some objects that represent as broad a range of tactile surfaces as possible—hard, soft, fuzzy, hairy, moist, slippery, warm, cool, etc. Close your eyes and feel each of these. Which one of them would you say is most like feelings of faith? Why?

"Since in the wisdom of God the world through its wisdom did not know him, God was pleased through the foolishness of what was preached to save those who believe" (1 Cor. 1:21, NIV).

Cleopas

He shook his head and wondered
if what he'd seen had actually happened.
The little group around the table
buzzed with excitement.
"I can't imagine,"
Cleopas said to another,
"how we could have walked with Him
all the way to Emmaus
without knowing!
It isn't as though we didn't
have clues enough.
Looking back,
I can recall a dozen little things
that should have told us
who He was."
Cleopas thumped his fist on the table.
"We were such fools!
Grumbling the whole way,
our heads down,
never once glancing up into His face.
A real look
was all we would have needed.

We were like children fretting

over what to do next,

and the solution

walked in sandals there with us."

    Tears of sheer wonder

flooded Cleopas' eyes,

and he could not help smiling.

Wiping the tears away

with the back of his hand,

he looked around the room

at the others.

The tension of the past week—

the gut-wrenching agony and death,

the ash-gray face

as they lay the body in the tomb—

had vanished for them all in a flash

of sweet recognition.

    "I guess it's little wonder

that we didn't know Him,"

Cleopas said with a sigh.

"We've been so wrong

about everything else."

↻ Explain in your own words the meaning of the phrase "the foolishness of what was preached."

↻ List "a dozen little things" that increase your faith in Jesus.

↻ Look up *faith* in a thesaurus. Think about which words connect most clearly to your understanding of faith as it is exercised by a Christian.

"[All] are justified freely by [God's] grace through the redemption that came by Christ Jesus" (Rom. 3:24, NIV).

It Isn't Hype!

The first known written advertisement is a 3,000-year-old "wanted poster" that archaeologists have found in Thebes, Egypt. It offers the reward of a gold coin for the return of a runaway slave named Shem.

Since that time poster advertising in public places was used frequently throughout the Middle Ages to offer a variety of goods. Then about 1450, after the invention of the printing press with movable type, advertising really took off in posters and newspapers. By the middle of the eighteenth century it had become such an everyday occurrence in society that Samuel Johnson wrote: "Advertisements are now so numerous that they are very negligently perused, and it is therefore become necessary to gain attention by magnificence of promise and by eloquence sometimes sublime and sometimes pathetick."

Today, of course, the advertising industry has us virtually surrounded. Everywhere you look, "sublime" and "pathetick" messages bombard us from every direction. In newspapers, magazines, books, billboards, posters, bumper stickers, radio, television, motion pictures, and Web pages, we are subjected to the "magnificence of promise."

And when we're exposed to—and disappointed by—so many promises in today's media, it's only human nature to become cynical. Considering that all these messages are motivated by self-gain, it takes a measure of faith to accept the "magnificence of promise" that all who accept God's offer of salvation "are justified freely by his grace through the redemption that came by Christ Jesus."

↪ Explain in your own words the "magnificence of [God's] promise."

↪ From a human standpoint, why is it difficult to accept the idea that we "are justified freely by [God's] grace"?

↪ Analyze three full-page print advertisements from a magazine. Think about the ways in which these advertisements attempt to influence what a reader places his or her faith in.

Day 6

"The Lord redeems his servants; no one will be condemned who takes refuge in him" (Ps. 34:22, NIV).

Mount Ararat

The animals were gone—
at long last!
All that hooting
   and growling
      and screeching
        and trumpeting.
Now only silence
   whistled lightly around the end
      of the great ramshackle ship,
   moaned in desolation.
Noah looked out
   across the new
   green-sweet valleys
   radiating southward
   into the blue haze—

a new world

left for him and his

alone to people.

Whither the first step?

Where to begin?

Noah smiled knowingly

at the uncertainty,

returning as it had

for the hundred twenty years.

The old assurance

flushed his cheeks,

hot and pink and tingling.

Noah was good at uncertainties;

they didn't bother him at all.

The only thing he knew for sure

was that it would

all work out.

He had his multicolored promise,

and that was enough for him.

↻ In what way did the "multicolored promise" involve faith?

↻ What practical steps can be taken to overcome uncertainty in God's leading?

↻ Talk to a friend about what in life strengthens his or her faith most.

Day 7

"Do not throw away your confidence; it will be richly rewarded" (Heb. 10:35, NIV).

Making It Personal

Try some of the following activities as you complete this week's consideration of the subject of faith:

↺ Begin to make your own computer database to include a variety of media that enrich your faith in God.

↺ List 10 physical objects that you would place in a time capsule to express your faith in God.

↺ Read the chapter "Faith and Acceptance" in *Steps to Christ*.

↺ In some art form (drawing, painting, sculpture, etc.), produce your own representation of the concept of faith.

↺ Read some of the responsive readings on the subject of faith and trust in *The Seventh-day Adventist Hymnal* (numbers 698, 799, 800). Think about how these readings affect your personal faith.

Judging

"You have no excuse, whoever you are, when you judge others; for in passing judgment on another you condemn yourself, because you, the judge, are doing the very same things" (Rom. 2:1, NRSV).

The Real Issue

The members of the church at Bulldog Heights weren't your everyday, run-of-the-mill congregation. No way! Not this group of believers. When they saw a problem with the way things were being run in their church, they went right after it teeth first. No beating around the bush for this bunch.

In fact, that's why someone at a church board meeting one night brought up the issue of jewelry. If ever there was a topic that sparked instant discussion, this seemed to be it. Atomic fission could not have set off a more volatile debate. And, interestingly enough, there *didn't* seem to be any disagreement over the gravity of the problem. Such was the unanimity of the Bulldog Heights church board. The real controversy centered, rather, on what exactly should be done about "this obscene encroachment of rampant paganism itself into the vulnerable inner recesses of our very midst," as one outraged member put it. "Pierced ears indeed!" he cried. "Next thing you know they'll be piercing their noses and who knows what else! I ask you: 'Is this any way for a

Christian to groom himself—herself—er, whatever!'"

To some, the obvious solution appeared to be expunging from the church rolls the names of "jewelry junkies," a term that some clever wag coined just for the occasion. But others pointed out that taking someone's membership away wouldn't necessarily prevent him or her from attending church anyway. "That's the kind of audacity we're dealing with here," she said with a sniff.

One pugnacious board member suggested the idea of placing two burly deacons at each entrance to the building to turn away anyone wearing jewelry who tried to storm the place. But then the chair observed that inspections could get to be a little, well, indelicate. Young girls—and boys, too, for that matter—could hide their pierced ears under long hair that someone would have to lift aside to check. Well, the mention of long hair derailed the discussion a full half hour before the board chair could get everyone settled down and back on track.

It was at this moment that the idea of an electronic jewelry alarm bubbled to the surface of the deliberation. The boardroom fell silent in a collective thrill. Here was a genuine out-of-the-blue twenty-first-century example of inspiration if ever there was one. So thorough. So dispassionate. So *perfect!*

It took a little more than six months for the board to find a system that claimed to do the job adequately. In the meantime the board members sat in their usual places in the pews with smug smiles. *The time is coming,* they thought, *when we'll be able to weed all these "jewelry junkies" from our midst. Their day will come.*

At last one morning everything was in place. The jewelry alarms had been installed *and* the aforementioned burly deacons stationed at each entrance. The word had gone out the week before that no one—*no one*—would be allowed in the sanctuary without passing through the jewelry alarm. No exceptions—period. It didn't take very long to put the new system to the test.

Chaos.

Bells and whistles and sirens and flashing red lights. Belt

buckles, watches, tie pins, brooches, barrettes, money clips, pens, compacts, key chains—you name it. Whatever was made of metal set off the alarms. When it was all over, only 14 people got through, and they looked around at one another in bewilderment. Not one of the deacons themselves passed the test. "Well," one of them commented, "there goes this morning's program, I guess."

There goes the program indeed! It was a chastened bunch of members who met in the emergency board meeting that evening in Bulldog Heights. Two or three made a few attempts to trace responsibility for the idea of a jewelry alarm, but all they accomplished was more confusion and the suspicion that it was they themselves who had started the whole fiasco.

Well, now what? Fortunately, the board members made the only inspired decision they'd made in months. They knelt together and asked for God's leading through the valley of the shadow of darkness that they'd created for themselves. And after much further discussion—and prayer—they decided that the best thing would be to "beat the jewelry alarms into plow shares," as one person expressed it. "We've been worrying about changing other people," he said, "but I guess we'd better take a little closer look at how we might change ourselves."

↪ To what extent, if any, should a congregation attempt to seek uniformity among its members?

↪ How does someone overcome the temptation to judge others? Be specific.

↪ In prayer, ask God to show you ways in which judging others may be a problem for you, and ask Him to help you overcome it.

"Judge nothing before the appointed time; wait till the Lord comes. He will bring to light what is hidden in darkness and will expose the motives of men's hearts. At that time each will receive his praise from God" (1 Cor. 4:5, NIV).

My List

Let's see now . . .

Surely Mr. Lindemann

will go to heaven—

He has such a singing voice

as angels would envy

if they could;

and the old Johnson couple,

bless their hearts—

imagine, married 60 years;

and the thin, young lady—

what's her name?—

Alice Enders,

Always gets her "Jasper Wayne"

(even in December blizzards);

and Dr. Cicarelli

single-handedly, they say,

donated half the cost

of the new church narthex

seven years ago.

There's something satisfying

and unsettling in a list:

I wonder if my name's

    on anybody else's,

yet down deep

    I know it shouldn't really matter.

↪ How does "My List" relate to the idea that a Christian should "judge nothing before the appointed time"?

↪ What is the difference between making a list, like the one in the poem, and looking up to other Christians for inspiration?

↪ Find an example of a time when Jesus complimented someone for doing something worthwhile. Think about how He went about doing this.

Day 3

"The Son of man is come to seek and to save that which was lost"
(Luke 19:10).

Are You Out of Your Tree?

Every year since 1970 the people of Cohocton, New York, have held a weekend tree- sitting contest. The object is to see who can stay in a tree the longest with the least amount of gear.

Each contestant is weighed in before climbing into the tree. Some don't take anything; others take as much as 35 pounds of equipment—such things as a hammock, food, seat belt— one participant even took along his homework.

Contestants are penalized for trips to the bathroom and disqualified if they drop anything. One attempted to cut down on bathroom trips by not drinking for three days before the contest. Another skipped all meals the day before. And all this for a grand prize of $200.

This is kind of the opposite of the experience of Zacchaeus.

This pint-sized tax collector had to take to a sycamore tree to see over the crowd. When Jesus saw him there, he told Zacchaeus to come down out of the tree, and invited Himself to Zacchaeus' house for dinner.

"Jesus has some extraordinarily peculiar sheep: some that are unkempt and dirty, some that are awkward or pushy, and some that have gone astray!" writes Oswald Chambers in *My Utmost for His Highest*. "But it is impossible to exhaust God's love."

This really raised the eyebrows of the bystanders, who thought it was a big mistake to go to the house of so obvious a sinner. But Jesus took the opportunity to point out that it was for just such sinners that He'd come to earth. To Jesus, saving sinners is a contact sport.

Unlike the people of Cohocton, New York, Zacchaeus was the big winner for coming down out of his tree. Most of the onlookers at the time didn't even understand the rules of the game.

↪ How is saving sinners a contact sport?

↪ How could it be said that judging others is a "noncontact" sport?

↪ Observe some kind of competition in which judging is a part— a dog show, athletic event, cookoff, etc. Think about the similarities and differences of this competition with the way in which church members sometimes judge one another.

"There is only one Lawgiver and Judge, the one who is able to save and destroy. But you—who are you to judge your neighbor?" (James 4:12, NIV).

The Woman at the Well

The door swung open,
clattering against the wall,
and the woman hurried in.
A man rolled over on the bed,
scowling in the sudden sunlight.
"Where is your jar?" he asked.
"I thought you'd gone for water."
The woman's face glowed
with the heat of the waning afternoon—
or was it something else?
He couldn't tell.
"I have no further need for water,"
she said breathlessly.
He rolled his eyes.
"You and your riddles."
She laughed.
"I've seen the Messiah."
The man looked at her more closely.
"Have you indeed?
You went out for water
and you found the Messiah."
"He is at Jacob's well."

"Just sitting there,
passing the afternoon, is he?"

The woman turned abruptly serious.
"Don't mock me!
I know what I've seen."

"Why are you so sure
that he is the Messiah?" the man asked.

"He knows my whole life.
He knows of my marriages.
He knows of you and me . . ."

"Everyone in Sychar
knows of you and me;
there's nothing remarkable in that."

"But no one else has known
the desperation we've admitted
only to each other—
the times we've clung together,
weeping in the darkness."

The man turned away.
"You swore you would never
tell anyone of that."

She sat down next to him—
reached out and touched his shoulder.
"I didn't tell Him; He told me.
It seems He knows us
better than we know ourselves.
He knows what we want—
what we *really* want."

"What *do* we really want?"

"You will know that

when you see Him."

"I am not a religious man . . ."

She took his hand

and led him toward the door.

"That is just the part

that is most thrilling—

neither is He."

↪ In what ways had the woman at the well been judged by others?

↪ How should one respond to the judgment of others?

↪ Ask someone you know with experience in counseling to suggest several ways you can learn to become less judgmental of others.

Day 5

"God is no respecter of persons" (Acts 10:34).

Twelve Ordinary Men

British author G. K. Chesterton was an outspoken champion of common people. After serving as a jury member, Chesterton wrote, "Our civilization has decided, and very justly decided, that determining the guilt or innocence of men is a thing too important to be trusted to trained men. . . . When it wants a library catalogued, or the solar system discovered, or any trifle of that kind, it uses its specialists. But when it wishes anything done which is really serious, it collects 12 of the ordinary men standing round. The same thing was done, if I remember right, by the Founder of Christianity."

And that is something we too often forget. If Jesus hadn't come to earth 2,000 years ago, but came now instead, we'd probably expect Him to select the leadership for His new church from people like those on the cover of *Time* and *Newsweek*. Who better to be leaders? But Jesus' criterion for leadership in the early Christian church was, quite simply, belief. That's something that the celebrities of His time had trouble with. We may think that Jesus disqualified the elite of Jerusalem from leadership in His fledgling organization, but it's likelier that they disqualified themselves. After all, if Jesus is truly "no respecter of persons," He certainly would never turn away even a person with a Ph.D.

↪ To what was Chesterton referring when he said, "The same thing was done, if I remember right, by the Founder of Christianity"?

↪ In what ways is Jesus' evaluation of a person different from the evaluation of the rest of humanity?

↪ Read Acts 10:34 and paraphrase it in your own words. Meditate on this text for a time, thinking about how you can communicate its message to others through your own life.

Day 6

"Accept him whose faith is weak, without passing judgment on disputable matters" (Rom. 14:1, NIV).

Christianity Café

The sign in the window says,

"All you can eat for free!"

I can smell the fresh-baked bread

from clear across the street—

heavenly!

So I figure,

Why not give it a try—

the price is right.

Been looking for my food too long

in dark dead ends and alleyways.

Pushing the front door open,

I walk in as though I owned the place

and ask to see a menu.

You would have thought

I'd pulled the fire alarm.

How was I to know

there was a dress code?

Don't they know

the poorest dressed are hungriest?

Yet I'm starved enough to wonder,

If I don't belong in the dining room,

would they let me eat in the kitchen?

Do they serve take-out?

↻ In spiritual terms, explain the meaning of the following: "Don't they know the poorest dressed are hungriest?"

↻ Why do you think people are so uncomfortable with the differences they see in others?

↻ Compare and contrast the message of "Christianity Café" with that of "Dress Code" (see page 28).

Day 7

"Do not judge, or you too will be judged. For in the same way you judge others, you will be judged, and with the measure you use, it will be measured to you" (Matt. 7:1, 2, NIV).

Making It Personal

Try some of the following activities as you complete this week's consideration of the subject of judging:

↺ Next time you are in church, look for someone who appears to feel awkward or out of place. Invite him or her out to dinner during the coming week so you can become better acquainted.

↺ Think of three object lessons from nature that illustrate the importance of accepting others as they are.

↺ Create your own puppet show in which you communicate to children the importance of accepting others. Offer to present the show to children in your church.

↺ Read the chapter "Tares" in *Christ's Object Lessons*.

↺ Select a character from the New Testament to whom Jesus showed unexpected acceptance, and write a monologue or dialogue like "The Woman at the Well" in which you show this character's imagined response to Jesus' love.

Self-esteem 7

"I am fearfully and wonderfully made; your works are wonderful, I know that full well" (Ps. 139:14, NIV).

Fredd's Recipe for Happiness

At first Fredd was pretty well pleased to be a gingerbread man. With some amusement, he looked around Welkin's Wonders Bakery Shop at tray upon tray of the widest variety of bakery goods imaginable. What strange creations they all were! He chuckled at the chocolate eclairs, cackled at the coconut macaroons, and snickered at the snicker doodles. After considering their unusual flavors and forms and colors, Fredd concluded that he was glad he had not been made like them. His red cinnamon buttons swelled his vest with pride.

But then it didn't take too much longer for him to notice the other gingerbread men in the bakery shop window. They were easily the most popular in the shop, but there had to be at least five or six dozen of them in Welkin's Wonders, and every one had been made identical: two raisin eyes in the face and two red cinnamon buttons on the vest. It was positively monotonous. *I'm going to be different from the rest,* he resolved. *I'm going to find a way to stand out in this crowd.* Fredd wanted to be one of a kind.

As it happens, however, gingerbread men don't have much

opportunity to distinguish themselves from other gingerbread men around them. They all are made of the same basic ingredients—flour, water, spices, sugar. They all take their form from the same basic cookie cutter. They all spend a basic 12 minutes in the oven at 350°F. They all go into the baker's window to be sold for 59 cents. "Basic," Fredd muttered grumpily to himself. "After all is said and done, I'm only basic!"

He felt powerless. He couldn't add a third cinnamon button to his vest or a third raisin for a nose. He was taken out of the oven at the same time as 11 others of his kind on the cookie sheet, so he didn't have the option of staying a little longer to work on his tan. In an environment like that, it's tough to be unique.

And what upset Fredd even more was that he wanted to do something important with his life. He thought that a gingerbread man should be able to make something of himself, rather than have the baker make something of him. He wanted to become the greatest gingerbread man who ever rose out of the obscurity of Welkin's Wonders. He wanted to accomplish something with his life. Fredd's greatest wish was to be a self-made gingerbread man.

But late in the afternoon he was still lying in his place in the bakery shop window, wondering how in the world he was going to distinguish himself. By now the chocolate eclairs and snicker doodles were sold out completely, and almost all the gingerbread men were gone. It was getting on toward closing time, and Fredd was worried.

Then a little boy stopped by on the sidewalk in front of the bakery shop. The kid didn't look like much—knees wearing through his trousers, dirty baseball cap, ragged sweatshirt. Fredd watched anxiously as the boy peered through the window, thrust his grubby fists into his pockets, and pulled out some change. He saw him count the few coins in his hand to see if he had 59 cents.

With a tingle of anticipation, Fredd waited as the little boy shuffled into the shop, put his money on the counter, and pointed directly at him. This was going to be his moment at last! The baker took up Fredd with a spatula, wrapped him in wax paper, and slipped him into a neat white paper sack.

Whistling a happy tune to himself, the little boy skipped out of the bakery shop and down the street. Moments later he stopped on a street corner and pulled Fredd out of the sack. Looking him directly in his raisin eyes, the boy said, "OK, your name is Fredd, spelled with two d's. Well, when it came down to it, Fredd hadn't realized that he had been nameless back at Welkin's Wonders. There in the bakery shop, it had always been "Hey, you!" Nobody ever took the time to name every gingerbread man in the place.

The boy put Fredd back in the sack and carried him all the way home. As Fredd rattled around in his comfortable new paper sack, he began to feel a warmth he hadn't experienced since he'd left the oven back at Welkin's Wonders. *Maybe being basic isn't so bad a thing,* he decided. *Even though I may be pretty much like every other gingerbread man in the bakery shop, I'm the only one in this kid's life.*

And that's no half-baked idea!

↪ State in your own words what Fredd learned about self-esteem in this parable.

↪ How would you answer someone's comment that he or she is "only basic"?

↪ Make a list of 10 positive facts about yourself that make you unique.

Day 2

"What are human beings that you are mindful of them, mortals that you care for them? Yet you have made them a little lower than God, and crowned them with glory and honor" (Ps. 8:4, 5, NRSV).

Merely Blue

Once there was a stained-glass window
　　depicting Jesus bowed—exhausted—
　　　　beneath the rough-grained weight
　　　　　　of two beams crossed upon His back.
One sunny Tuesday afternoon
　　the church was still and organ silent,
　　the shards of glass were analyzing
　　　　merits of the colored patches
　　　　　　they were casting on the carpet.
One small chip of scarlet,
　　seeing Jesus' deep, rich purple robe,
　　said he wished
　　　　that he could change his role—
　　　　　　become a purple, maybe, too.
A blue triangle
　　smiled understandingly and said,
　　　　"I once pined to be a yellow,
　　　　　　something more intense
　　　　　　than merely blue, at least.
　　　　But since that time I've come to realize
　　　　　　that ochre, puce, or crimson
　　　　　　have no virtue of their own.

By now I've learned to be content

to let the sun

invest me with intensity."

↪ "Ochre, puce, or crimson have no virtue of their own." How would you state this idea in spiritual terms?

↪ What does the poem "Merely Blue" suggest about Christian self-esteem?

↪ Visit a church in your community with a stained-glass window. Spend some time studying the window, and select one piece of glass that you think represents your place in your environment. Think about why you've selected that piece. Before you leave, read the last lines of the poem "Merely Blue."

Day 3

"I am the vine; you are the branches. If a man remains in me and I in him, he will bear much fruit; apart from me you can do nothing" (John 15:5, NIV).

Getting in Too Deep

At the peak of his career, world heavyweight champion Muhammad Ali was particularly noted for his cockiness. One day on an airplane, just before takeoff, a flight attendant came down the aisle and reminded him to fasten his seat belt.

"Superman don't need no seat belt," Ali grumbled.

"Superman don't need no airplane, either," the flight attendant retorted.

With a smile of chagrin, Ali buckled his seat belt.

Sometimes Christians make the same mistake as Muhammad Ali. After a certain amount of outward success, they think they're Superman. They forget that it is God who has given them the abilities and opportunities to achieve their goals. They come to think that they are solely responsible for what they have accomplished.

Consider Peter's experience on the Sea of Galilee. In the midst of a howling storm the disciples were doing everything they could possibly do to save themselves. Just at the time when all seemed lost, someone spotted Jesus walking on the heaving waves. Frightened, they all thought He was a ghost. "Take courage," Jesus said. "It is I."

"If it's you," Peter said, "let me come to you on the water."

When Jesus beckoned for him to come, Peter stepped out of the boat and actually walked on the surface of the Sea of Galilee. What he was doing was a rare accomplishment, but he looked at the event from a human viewpoint. He forgot momentarily that Jesus was the power behind his out-of-boat experience.

When Christians forget where their accomplishment comes from, they are certainly in over their heads. But if they continue to recognize God's influence in their lives, God will make them champions.

- Are humility and positive self-esteem mutually exclusive? Explain your answer.

- How should the decision to give your life to Jesus affect your self-esteem? Explain your answer.

- Read a feature magazine article about a professional athlete. What does this article suggest about the development of positive self-esteem?

"You both precede and follow me, and place your hand of blessing on my head. This is too glorious, too wonderful to believe!" (Ps. 139:5, 6, TLB).

Mary and Martha

Martha stood in the doorway
with her fists on her hips,
glaring at her sister
who dreamily watched
the sun slip down
to touch the waiting hills.
"Someday He's going
to see right through you, Mary—
all the fawning and sighing,
and those big, innocent eyes of yours.
Then maybe He'll notice
the work I've gone to,
making things nice around here."
Mary did not like to fight.
"You're right," she said.
"When He is here,
I only want to sit
and listen to His stories.
My usefulness flies out the window."
She shook her head and sighed.
"He told me He's going to die soon.
It sounded to me

as though He wanted company and quiet
more than bread and drink."

Martha read her sister's face,
and her anger crumbled
like the walls of Jericho.
She passed a trembling hand
across her forehead,
her usual composure stricken.
"How could I have been so wrong?" she moaned.
"Will He ever forgive me?"

Mary smiled.
"Of course He will;
He already has.
It doesn't matter
what we've done or haven't done.
He loves us all—
the doers and the dreamers."

⟳ In your own words, explain the reassurance of the statement "You both precede and follow me."

⟳ From the dialogue between Mary and Martha above, what could each of the sisters have taught the other about self-esteem?

⟳ Think about Jesus' self-esteem. Write down at least three experiences from His life that show the source of His positive self-esteem.

"Are not two sparrows sold for a farthing? and one of them shall not fall on the ground without your Father. But the very hairs of your head are all numbered" (Matt. 10:29, 30).

A Sparrow's Fall

Eastern screech owls have adapted well to civilization. After more than two decades studying this interesting bird, ecologist Frederick Gehlbach of Baylor University has made some fascinating discoveries.

Completely at ease in the world of humans, cars, and pets, the Eastern screech owl actually does better in suburbs than in its natural environment. Because human communities provide an abundance of bugs, birds, and snakes, this adaptable little owl has actually become five times more numerous in the suburbs than it is in the wild.

Gehlbach has also discovered that it has a fascinating way of keeping its nest tidy. It captures small blind snakes and drops them into the hollow of the tree in which it has made its nest. There the snakes live among the Eastern screech owl chicks, eating the various insects that live in the rather messy chick droppings. This, in turn, seems to help protect the chicks from the diseases that are carried by these various kinds of insects. In fact, Gehlbach says that in a snake-sanitized nest the owlets grow significantly faster and survive in greater numbers than those in nests without the small serpents. And, even more interestingly, although Eastern screech owls have a great taste for small snakes, they choose not to eat these small blind snakes because, apparently, they are particularly useful.

God has such an interest in every species of animal in our world that He created special relationships among certain species. The Eastern screech owl helps to maintain the balance of nature in our neighborhoods. The small blind snakes provide them with somewhat the same service.

If God considers these small creatures to be important enough to create special relationships between them, how much more He must think of us. We are told that He has numbered the very hairs of our head. If He notices when a sparrow falls, He surely must care that much more when we fall. That's why He sent His Son to die in our place.

↷ Why do you think Jesus chose so plentiful and insignificant an animal as a sparrow to illustrate God's love for us?

↷ How does the certainty of God's love affect someone in everyday ways?

↷ Take time to observe the behavior of some birds in your neighborhood. As you do so, meditate on your importance to God as described in Matthew 10:29, 30.

Day 6

"The Lord does not see as mortals see; they look on the outward appearance, but the Lord looks on the heart" (1 Sam. 16:7, NRSV).

Does Not Compute

My poor computer, overtaxed,

says it ran out of decimals

in estimating what

the chances of my being are—

my probability.

My parents may have never met

or never cared much for each other

(a near miss, nothing more).

> I could have gone at life
>> with someone else's DNA,
>>> who would have had
>>>> to muddle through
>>>>> with someone else's, who . . .
>> I guess I could consider me
>>> just a happy accident—
>>>> unlikely as a platypus—
>>>>> if life were proved statistically.

↪ Does 1 Samuel 16:7 imply that Christians need not concern themselves with dress and grooming? Explain your answer.

↪ The poem "Does Not Compute" deals with an old philosophical question: Why am I here? State in your own words how you think the poem answers this question.

↪ Talk to a close friend about ways in which you can bolster one another's positive self-esteem. Decide together on a quiet campaign to help each other in this way.

Day 7

"Jesus Christ laid down his life for us" (1 John 3:16, NIV).

Making It Personal

Try some of the following activities as you complete this week's consideration of the subject of self-esteem:

↺ For at least a week, keep a journal in which you record your feelings about yourself. Think about specific techniques you can use to improve your feelings about yourself when they are negative.

↷ Read the chapter "Rejoicing in the Lord" in *Steps to Christ*.

↷ Observe some professional athletes in a sporting event on TV. Think about what their behavior suggests about positive self-esteem. List some scriptural verses that come to mind as you conduct this project?

↷ Explore the Iternet and analyze several *personal* home pages. Consider what these home pages suggest about the self-esteem of the people who have created them.

↷ After reviewing the poem "Merely Blue," create a stained-glass project of your own that expresses your focus on God as the center of your positive self-esteem.

Love

Day 1

"God demonstrates his own love for us in this: While we were still sinners, Christ died for us" (Rom. 5:8, NIV).

The Innkeeper

The innkeeper looked up from totaling his accounts for the day and squinted nearsightedly at the figure standing in the doorway of the inn. Sure enough, there, with his shadow cast longways across the room, was that crazy Samaritan again. He really hadn't expected him to return, even though he'd solemnly promised that he would.

The innkeeper straightened up and folded his arms before him. "So," he said shaking his head in disbelief, "you have come back after all!"

A look of puzzlement crossed the Samaritan's face. "Of course," he said. "I wanted to be sure to follow up, to make certain that the fellow I left with you last week is feeling better."

"Oh, he's better, all right," the innkeeper said. "I would say he's doing just fine physically, but he was one of the most unlikable people I've ever met. I have had to serve all kinds of unpleasant people in my work, but I have to tell you that I came very close at least twice to throwing him out in the street and refusing to care for him any longer."

"Was he trouble for you?"

"*Trouble* is too mild a word for that arrogant rascal. I caught myself thinking now and again that I'd have liked to been out there on the road and thumped him a time or two myself!"

The Samaritan burst out a laugh so musical that it somehow unaccountably touched the innkeeper's heart, and he realized for the first time why he had been so forbearing with the injured man, why he hadn't indeed thrown him out into the street.

"He left two days ago while I was cleaning another room, pilfered two of my best towels and just slipped away without so much as a goodbye."

"I said I would reimburse you for whatever was needed. I'll gladly pay you for the towels. Do I owe you anything more for his care?" the Samaritan asked.

"No, he didn't stay as long as we thought he may need to. Do you know he had the audacity to say he was leaving early and demanded that I give him the unused balance of the money you'd left for his care?"

"You could have given it to him," the Samaritan said. "I have plenty, and it may be that he needed it for something."

The innkeeper could contain himself no longer. As a businessman he'd made it his policy to tend only to his own affairs. That's what best suited in the kind of place he worked. You didn't have to be a doctor of letters to see that someone seeking a room had unseemly things in mind for it. But now he had to ask his question.

"You do know, don't you, that that wretch would never have even considered doing the same thing for you. *Gratitude* just isn't in his lexicon. If the situation had been reversed, by now your carcass would have been picked clean by the buzzards out there in that God- forsaken country."

"Ah," the Samaritan said with a wan smile, "my carcass has indeed been picked clean many a time. And will be again, I'm sure." He sighed. "That, in fact, appears to be my purpose in life."

The innkeeper was a practical man who seldom pierced the literal crust of his everyday language. He simply didn't have time for such things. He looked at the Samaritan as though he were speaking an unknown foreign language, which indeed he was.

"I know that it's probable that he would not have done as much for me," the Samaritan said, "but what might have been is not the point. What *is* is all that is important. By the way, did he leave a forwarding address? I'd like to contact him."

The innkeeper began to laugh and then fell quickly silent in embarrassment. He hadn't meant to ridicule the Samaritan's naïveté. "No," he said. "I'm sorry, but he probably was trying to escape any obligation to you."

"I suspect you're right," the Samaritan said. "But he does have my address. I gave it to him when I left last week. Whatever happens, I think we'll cross paths again someday. I'll be watching for him."

↻ How does the expression "while we were yet sinners" relate to the injured man in "The Innkeeper"?

↻ How should Christians respond to ingratitude from those they have served?

↻ "The Innkeeper" is a sequel to one of Jesus' parables. Write a sequel of your own to a parable of Jesus.

Day 2

"I led them with cords of human kindness, with ties of love; I lifted the yoke from their neck and bent down to feed them" (Hosea 11:4, NIV).

Healing

They must have winced—
　　the twelve of them—
as Jesus spat upon the ground
　　and mixed the spittle
　　　　with the loose dust
　　　　　　of the roadway.
And then to dab it
　　on the beggar's eyes
　　as though it were a poultice
　　　　that some toothless old lady
　　　　　　had told Him about.
He didn't need the spittle-mud
　　any more than he needed water
　　　　to make the wedding wine
　　or five loaves and two fishes
　　　　to feed the milling multitude.
They knew that by now.
　　But they didn't know
　　　　He was trying to heal
　　　　　　their blindness as well.

↻ According to this poem, in what way was "the twelve of them" in need of healing?

- What connection is there, if any, between physical healing and spiritual healing?

- While you are blindfolded, listen to two or three recordings on cassette or CD of your favorite religious music. Pray that God will heal you of any spiritual blindness that may be affecting your relationship with Him.

"Then the owner of the vineyard said, 'What shall I do? I will send my son, whom I love; perhaps they will respect him'" (Luke 20:13, NIV).

Special Delivery

Seventy-seven-year-old R. V. Breese, of Chula Vista, California, checked his mailbox on a day in early November 1990. Among the bills and junk mail was a letter from his son, Denny, in the Navy. "This will be short," the letter said in part, "but I just found out that the mail is leaving the boat in about 15 minutes. I just want you to get this envelope that was stamped at the North Pole."

Seaman Denny Breese was a crew member aboard the nuclear-powered U.S.S. *Nautilus,* the first submarine to sail beneath the North Pole—in August 1958. The letter had taken 32 years to be delivered to his parents' home in California. Fortunately, they still lived at the same address.

"It's impossible to tell where it's been," said a postal service spokesperson in San Diego. "This happens occasionally."

We always appreciate communication from a loved one. But certainly this letter is treasured all the more by Denny Breese's family because of the length of time that it took to receive it.

About two thousand years ago God sent a letter to us by Special Delivery. It was His own Son, sent down to this earth to deliver a message of love. Unfortunately, only a handful of people recognized the true meaning and value of the message.

In a poem Emily Dickinson wrote, "This is my letter to the world/That never wrote to me." God must feel something like this. He is trying to communicate with us, and too often we are ignoring what is in our mailbox. Maybe it's time to open our mailbox and take a good look at its exciting contents.

↪ How do the lines above from the Emily Dickinson poem connect to the story "The Innkeeper" (see page 90)?

↪ How do you relate to the rejection of others?

↪ Get in touch today with someone whom you have neglected recently. Offer to do something specific together within the next week.

Day 4

"He lifts the burdens from those bent down beneath their loads" (Ps. 146:8, TLB).

The Demoniac

"Mother," he called

in a hoarse half-whisper.

"Let me in.

I promise I won't harm you."

The old woman's wary voice

came muffled through the heavy door.

"I cannot let you in;

you frighten me."

He trembled in the late evening.

The door squeaked open slightly,

and a blade of yellow light

bisected his face.

    "What do you want of me?" she asked.

    He didn't try to force his way;
she would expect that.
"I'm cold, Mother. May I come in?"

    She stepped back,
and the door creaked open on its own.
Retreating behind the table,
she resigned herself
to the worst he could do.

    He stepped in.
"Mother, I'm not the same anymore."

    She wrung her slender hands
and mumbled something to herself.

    "A man came to the tombs tonight.
I knew somehow
exactly who He was,
although I've never seen Him before.
I wanted to kill Him;
it made me grind my teeth
just to look at Him.

    "But with a simple word or two,
He flushed my wracking spirits out
and drove them into a herd of swine.
They ran themselves screaming into the lake
and left me standing, clean and empty
as a new-built house."

    Reaching out his hand
to his cowering mother,

he stepped toward her.

She searched his eyes
the way she'd done
countless times before.
Sometimes she could read his eyes,
and see the frightening storms
that howled inside his head.
But finding something there at last
she hadn't seen for many years,
she enfolded his hand in hers
and washed it with her tears.

☞ What examples of unconditional love do you find in "The Demoniac"?

☞ Define in your own words the expression "unconditional love."

☞ Find some object in your possession that best symbolizes love as you've experienced it personally. Place the object in a prominent place for a week to serve as a reminder of the importance of showing love to others.

Day 5

"I will pour water upon him that is thirsty, and floods upon the dry ground: I will pour my spirit upon thy seed, and my blessing upon thine offspring" (Isa. 44:3).

Drink Up!

In a forbidding place called Skeleton Coast Park, along the South Atlantic shores of Africa, lies a stretch of sand dunes and gravel plains as dry as anywhere in the world. Yet, although rain almost never falls there, researchers have discovered that small bands of elephants have developed ways of surviving the searing heat.

Sometimes going four days without finding any drinkable water, the elephants walk 30 miles at a stretch, looking for succulent plants that grow in dry riverbeds. They survive by eating these plants till they come across underground wells that they dig down to. Sometimes the water level is still out of reach of the smaller elephants. When this happens, the larger adults fill their trunks with water and pour it into the mouths of the calves. And the elephants' ability to dig these wells actually keeps other species alive, because after they leave, animals of many varieties gather to share in what they've found.

The life-giving qualities of pure water make it one of the most precious substances on earth. This is why water is used so frequently in the Bible to show God's loving care for us. He promised that if we put ourselves in His care, we will never be thirsty. He meant this physically and spiritually, and He proved it over and over as He led the children of Israel through the wilderness. We can enjoy the same benefits today if we share them with others. In his book *There and Back* George MacDonald writes, "That which cannot be freely shared can never be possessed."

↻ Why is water a universal symbol for blessings?

↻ In places in which water is plentiful, is its value as a symbol diminished? Explain your answer.

↻ Place before you a clear glass of water. List all the spiritual applications for water that you can think of. Be creative. And don't overlook the possibilities in its other forms: ice and steam.

Day 6

"By his power God raised the Lord from the dead, and he will raise us also" (1 Cor. 6:14, NIV).

Arrhythmia

On the darkest night of all,

the cosmos held its breath

in cardiac arrest,

unsure of its own life,

and monitored the flatline of its fate.

Its heart had stopped;

the next beat a cold eternity away:

a two-day death,

a chilling, morguelike calm.

And then, self-resuscitated,

began to beat again,

the rhythm stronger than before

and growing stronger still.

↻ Why is "self-resuscitated" so important to the theme of "Arrhythmia"?

↻ Why do you think the heart, a mere muscle, has been designated by many cultures as a symbol for love?

↻ In as quiet a place as available, take your own pulse for a full minute. Think about what the rhythm of your own heartbeat communicates about God's love to you personally.

"We love because he first loved us" (1 John 4:19, NIV).

Making It Personal

Try some of the following activities as you complete this week's consideration of the subject of love:

↻ Listen to two or three currently popular love songs. List the ways in which the lyrics of these songs differ from Scripture in their depiction of love.

↻ Read the chapters "God's Love for Man" in *Steps to Christ* and "Gethsemane" in *The Desire of Ages*.

↻ Select two or three scriptural references that you think express God's love in a special way, and send them without any explanation or elaboration as an e-mail message to all the people in your e-mail address book.

↻ Rewrite "The Innkeeper" in the form of a skit with three parts: a narrator, the innkeeper, and the Samaritan. Then, working with two friends, prepare to present this skit before an audience.

↻ Create a booklet of "love coupons" that contain promises of favors: "Good for one free back rub"; "Good for a free baby-sitting session"; "Good for a free ride when you need transportation," etc. Then give the booklet to someone you know who has been facing unusual trials in his or her life recently.

Righteousness

"Everyone who does what is right has been born of him" (1 John 2:29, NIV).

Pocket Philosophies

Pastor Bo Peep was losing his sheep and didn't know where to find them, but you have to give at least a measure of credit to the good clergyman for taking immediate action. The fact is, his flock had developed a gaping hole in its pocket—sheep and lambs kept falling out and never coming back to the fold again. It was a dismaying predicament for a pastor.

So he convened an open emergency meeting of the full church board. The entire congregation was invited. All the very best and brightest trooped into the boardroom that night. This was unquestionably going to be one of the pivotal board meetings in the history of Pastor Peep's fold, and no one wanted to be left out.

In his opening remarks Pastor Peep reviewed the development of his flock and outlined the problem to those in attendance. "This is a critical time for us," he said. "It has reached crisis proportions, and we simply must find a way to 'stop the fearful fallout,'" as he so colorfully described the problem to his listeners. "Does anyone have anything he or she would like to say?"

For a long, uncomfortable silence, all sat around the boardroom table ruminating. As everyone knows, sheep—especially in committees—have not often distinguished themselves for creativity or critical thinking. One crashing bolt of lightning, one piercing cry of a wolf, and they're completely frazzled.

At last, however, someone tentatively broke the stillness and got the ball rolling with a suggestion, something he'd heard once that sounded as though it had come from some deep thinking. "A stitch in time saves nine,'" he volunteered, and all the others mumbled their assent. Here indeed was wisdom in an hour of darkest need. All rose as one and headed for the door. Mission accomplished.

But then a brash young lamb—one of those egghead, overeducated types—quietly observed, "That particular aphorism applies more to saving stitches than to saving sheep."

Well, you'd think the young lamb had fouled the drinking water for the entire flock. All the members reluctantly returned to their places around the boardroom table. "We just can't let this be a simple solution, now, can we?" one muttered just loud enough to be heard throughout the room.

"I guess someone here," another grumbled, "hasn't learned to 'wear your learning, like your watch, in a *private* pocket,' as the saying goes!"

"Irrelevant again," the young lamb said, shaking his head. "Just how many of us these days still wear our watches in our pockets? That style went out a century ago."

Apparently at a stalemate, the group once again turned the somewhat questionable benefit of its thinking to the topic at hand. Another long silence.

"I have it!" another exclaimed after a few moments. "One rotten apple can spoil the whole barrel.'"

Ah, there you have it. With a triumphant glance in the direction of the egghead, the others mumbled their assent again. After all, there did seem to be more than enough assent to go around in this group.

"Nope," the young lamb said again. "That proverb isn't relevant to anything this board has discussed for a hundred years—if then!" Tact plainly wasn't his strong suit. "We're discussing pockets here," he added, "not barrels."

So, looking at one another in silent consternation, they tried to remember a proverb for a pocket. No one seemed to have had a grandmother or grandfather who had passed one down. Several could remember that one of their grandparents *had* passed kidney stones, but no relevant proverbs.

Then it was that one innocent in the workings of congregational politics, a somewhat new recruit, repeated a proverb that he'd heard in the pool halls of his youth, years before he'd ever considered joining Pastor Peep's flock, of course. After all, pool tables are supposed to have pockets, aren't they? But the group responded with such icy derision, such unmitigated scorn, that he almost secretly wished he himself could have slipped through the hole in the pocket at that very moment, if he could only find it.

In such a fractious atmosphere the evening wore on, board members bleating at one another across the table, with nobody hitting on any kind of workable resolution. And that may be why the solution, when it came, completely missed its mark.

At some time way past midnight, another young lamb quietly offered her opinion: "I think that the congregation should simply exchange its *holeyness* for *holiness*—"

In total exhaustion and exasperation, the group as one sent up a derisive whoop before she had a chance to spell the two words out for them. They completely missed a perfect opportunity to learn the difference between the two, and narrowly averted a happy ending.

↪ In your own words, explain the connection between *holeyness* and *holiness* in "Pocket Philosophies."

↪ In practical terms, how does a Christian attain holiness in his or her life?

Phone five fellow church members and ask them each to define *holiness*. How are their answers the same and how different?

"Ill-gotten gain brings no lasting happiness; right living does" (Prov. 10:2, TLB).

Being Cool

When I was 16,
    it was socially expedient
        to know Beatle's music,
        with its meanings hidden
        from the uninitiated:
            "Lucy in the Sky With Diamonds"
            was a grand inside joke
            that we guarded from our parents.
Farmer's daughter stories
    echoed in the locker room
        after basketball games,
and we grinned
    at the blank looks
        on freshman faces
        as they tried to sort out
            the double entendres
            and then laughed uncontrollably
                without really knowing why.
In fact, we learned a lot
    of worthless stuff

that few of us

had the courage *not* to learn.

And now, when I have to

sort through it all—

like cleaning a cluttered garage—

I wish I could have

the sweet mind

of a freshman again.

↪ How would you explain the difference between "right living" (Prov. 10:2, TLB) and righteousness by works?

↪ What is the basic human problem described by the narrator of "Being Cool"?

↪ Observe the behavior of some children at play. Consider the following question: How is a child's barriers to righteousness different from your own?

Day 3

"Resolve . . . never to put a stumbling block or hindrance in the way of another" (Rom. 14:13, NRSV).

Spin Control

In the latter part of 1982 *NBC Nightly News* broadcast for the first time an impressive new logo that featured a state-of-the-art computer animation of our beautiful blue earth spinning before the black backdrop of outer space. Within a few days, however, NBC began to receive a flood of letters, all pointing out that their earth was spinning backward—from east to west.

NBC had an explanation: it said that the logo was commissioned to depict the earth as it would be seen from the space shuttle that was then orbiting the earth 16 times a day from west to east, making it appear that the earth was spinning the other way. But the network received so many letters, including 14 postcards from a class of fifth graders in Sophia, West Virginia, that it finally gave up trying to explain. It couldn't simply run the tape backward, so it had to commission a brand-new animation—costing more than $50,000.

Sometimes Christians who read the biblical counsel that we are not to judge one another assume that we need not worry about how we conduct ourselves in the presence of others. "What I do," they assert, "is no one else's business." Not quite!

Caring Christians will always consider the influence of their conduct on others. It's always better to avoid doing something if it could lead another to go astray. Sometimes righteousness even means avoiding the acceptable thing if it is going to be "a stumbling block or hindrance in the way of another"!

↻ If sin is the breaking of the law, what law is broken when you do something that is "a stumbling block"? Explain your answer.

↻ How can someone know whether he or she is doing something that is "a stumbling block"?

↻ Write Romans 14:13 in your own words on an index card and use it as a bookmark for a while.

"The path of the godly leads to life" (Prov. 12:28, TLB).

The Disciples of John

"He *is* the Messiah," they reported.

"There is no doubt of it.

We have seen Him cast out demons,

give sight to the blind,

raise the dead."

John said nothing at first.

The deepening echo of the dungeon

oppressed them all;

desolation hung like a pall about them.

Somewhere water trickled over cold stones.

There was the crisp, harsh sound of marching feet.

Singing and laughter drifted distantly

from Herod's palace across the courtyard.

John sighed wearily.

"Of course, I've always known

He was the Messiah—

at least I've known

since the day I saw Him at the riverside.

There was in Him such a magnificent humility."

John nodded.

"I've known it since then."

He turned his tear-filled eyes toward them.

"It was you who needed convincing."

Then his eyes cleared and brightened,

took on the searing blue
that had pierced the hearts of hundreds
in the wilderness.

"You must follow Him—
wherever He leads you.
It won't be where you expect.
He has led me here—
to this clammy dungeon."
He shivered suddenly.
"But if I am to be here,
there is a purpose in it;
I'm sure of that."

The hollow clank of a huge key
in the door startled them.
The jailer burst officiously into the cell,
flanked by two dull, bristle-faced guards.

"Well, Baptist," the jailer sneered,
"it looks as though
you've preached your last sermon."
Motioning to the guards, he ordered,
"Take him away."

↪ What do you think is meant by the oxymoron "magnificent humility"?

↪ What three adjectives would you choose to describe John the Baptist's righteousness as it is depicted in this dialogue?

↪ Enclose yourself in a completely darkened room and imagine you are in John the Baptist's place in prison just before your execution. What scriptural passages come to mind that would give you encouragement to fight off feelings of abandonment?

"In every city the Holy Spirit warns me that prison and hardships are facing me. However, I consider my life worth nothing to me, if only I may finish the race and complete the task the Lord Jesus has given me—the task of testifying to the gospel of God's grace" (Acts 20:23, 24, NIV).

Rudely Interrupted

In the sixteenth century Fray Luis de León, of the Order of Saint Augustine, was elected at the age of 34 to a chair at Spain's University of Salamanca. He was widely respected as a theologian and immortalized as one of his nation's greatest poets.

Because Fray Luis was of Jewish descent, his rivals slandered him and accused him of heresy before the Inquisition. He was imprisoned in 1572, pending his trial. But the Inquisition wasn't particularly distinguished by its due process or swift justice.

He made repeated inquiries to the tribunal, asking of what he was charged so he could prepare a defense. As was the case in all Inquisition cases, witnesses were able to testify against him without divulging their identities.

At last, after an imprisonment of four years, eight months, and 19 days, he was freed with a reprimand, whereupon he returned to his teaching position and, it is said, opened his very first lecture with delicious defiance: "As I was saying before . . ."

Being tried for your religious beliefs is an almost completely alien concept to us today. But standing in the docket like a Luis de León or Martin Luther or John Huss isn't quite as foreign to us as we may at first think. In a sense, every Christian is on trial every day of his or her life. Forces of peer pressure, public opinion, and cultural influences are such that a Christian almost certainly will stand out. When that happens, God grant us each a measure of the courage of Luis de León.

- In what respects does a Christian's righteousness expose him or her to revilement or persecution where you live?

- How can a Christian know when to be defiant and when to conform?

- In prayer, thank God today for the freedom of religion that you have been granted.

Day 6

"We have all become like one who is unclean, and all our righteous deeds are like a filthy cloth" (Isa. 64:6, NRSV).

Animation

The wind animates a willow—
branches twist and reach
and grasp at each other.
Finger leaves flutter
in excited activity.
Without the wind,
the willow cannot move.
Jesus animates me—
as I sing, pray, and worship;
others, I hope, will see
my activity and know
I couldn't do it by myself.
Without Jesus,
I cannot move.

- What is the source of righteousness?

↪ If human righteousness is like a "filthy cloth," what is the first step to achieving true righteousness?

↪ Memorize at least three of the scriptural references in this week's readings.

"If anyone is in Christ, he is a new creation; the old has gone, the new has come!" (2 Cor. 5:17, NIV).

Making It Personal

Try some of the following activities as you complete this week's consideration of the subject of righteousness:

↻ Design a book jacket for an imaginary biography of the person in Scripture (other than Jesus) whom you think epitomizes righteousness. Include in the design the text for the back page that you hope would interest someone in reading your book.

↻ Read the chapter "Without a Wedding Garment" in *Christ's Object Lessons.*

↻ Select one of the scriptural references from this week's readings and feature it in your computer design for a small poster. Experiment with fonts, borders, images, textures, etc. Place the poster where it can serve as a reminder of the importance of righteousness.

↻ In a library or on the Internet, conduct a research project into religious persecution in the world today. Select a victim or victims of persecution and commit them to your personal prayer campaign on their behalf.

↻ Select an object lesson from nature to illustrate humanity's dependence on God for righteousness. Using this as a focus, write a short psalm of your own.

Goals

"The human mind plans the way, but the Lord directs the steps"
(Prov. 16:9, NRSV).

A Loop or a Straight Line

Cedric the Cessna was a little airplane, but he was growing and learning more each day. In fact, his fondest hope was that he would someday become a huge airliner that would work for United Airlines or British Airways. He would take people to exciting places all over the world. He dreamed of touching down in airports in Tahiti and Rio de Janeiro and Beijing and Stockholm.

But one day he kind of got into a playful mood and, just on a lark, tried a barrel roll. It was fun, so he tried a loop the loop. This gave him a funny feeling in the pit of his baggage compartment, but he liked it. As it turned out, he became so interested in stunt flying that he lost his interest in becoming an airliner.

"Who needs traffic control, anyway?" Cedric asked a friend one day. "All the tower does is give me a bunch of orders that I'm supposed to follow. It destroys my self-expression, my freedom! How can I truly get to know myself when I'm taking orders from the tower all the time? How can I get to know what's best for *me*?"

So Cedric began to experiment more and more. He tried new techniques that caused dizziness in the control panel and a flopping sensation in the cargo hold. His friends worried about him, of course, and they warned him of the dangers of stunt flying. He heard occasionally of other aircraft who, while doing the stunts, had crashed into lakes or mountainsides.

"Just poor judgment," Cedric said, dismissing his friends' concerns for him. "That's the trouble. If those planes had exercised a little more judgment, they could have learned to do barrel rolls and loop the loops responsibly. I'm in control of myself at all times. I can handle it. There's no need to worry."

But then one day something happened to Cedric. No, he didn't crash—as you might expect. Something happened that gently woke him up, that set the dials in his control panel to spinning entirely in a new direction. Just as he was about to leave the airport for another afternoon of fun in the great blue sky, a trim Lear jet swooped seemingly out of nowhere and touched lightly down on the Tarmac. The sleek, powerful jet happened to taxi right by Cedric as he was waiting for his turn to take off.

There was something about the Lear jet that immediately caught the little airplane's attention. He had a purposeful look, an air about him that said he knew where he was going.

"Where are you from?" Cedric asked in an attempt to make conversation.

"Just in from London," the Lear jet answered. "And what a time we had there! Where are you off to?"

Cedric gulped. For the first time in a long while he remembered his former goal of going to places like Tahiti and Rio de Janeiro and Beijing and Stockholm. He hadn't been as far as the city limits, much less to one of those exotic places on the map. "Just going up for a little spin," he said. "No place special. I'm going to try a few hammerhead stalls today."

"Are you kidding?" the Lear jet asked. "Sounds pretty dangerous to me. And besides, there are places I want to go. The stunts may be thrilling for a while, but when you're through, you're right back at the same airport. Have you ever noticed that? You're not going anywhere at all. That's not the kind of life for me!"

Cedric hadn't ever thought about stunt flying that way before. He had to admit that barrel rolls weren't taking him anywhere he really wanted to go. And he also had to admit that stunts could be dangerous. After a while you tended to get used to a stunt, and it didn't have the same excitement it once had. Then you'd do something to make it more exciting. And that made it even more dangerous.

Then Cedric remembered something the flight instructor had repeated several times in navigating class: "A straight line is the shortest distance between two points." *If I'm ever going to get to places like Tahiti or Rio,* the little airplane thought, *maybe I'd better begin to fly straight.*

And that's what he did. He began with a flight plan to the seat of the neighboring county. That went pretty well. When he arrived, he felt for the first time in a long while that he had accomplished something important. It wasn't London, exactly, but he had set a goal and achieved it. From that day on, Cedric adopted a completely new philosophy: Just Fly Straight! And before long, he was really going places.

↻ Does Proverbs 16:9 suggest that our planning is futile because God is directing our lives, or that our direction in life is the result of a partnership between us and God? Explain your answer.

↻ To what extent should a Christian rely on God for setting goals in life?

↻ Interview a member of your church congregation whom you consider to be successful. Discuss how the establishment of goals has affected his or her life.

"Just as you received Christ Jesus as Lord, continue to live in him, rooted and built up in him, strengthened in the faith as you were taught, and overflowing with thankfulness" (Col. 2:6, 7, NIV).

Got a Dime?

A young Camden, Arkansas, teenager named David, enchanted by movie scenes of Washington, D.C., determined that he would seek appointment as a congressional page. He went immediately to work on his goal, got the job, and enjoyed his work so much that he set another goal. This time he aimed somewhat higher: to return someday as a full-fledged member of the U.S. Congress.

As a personal gesture of his dream, David secretly hid a dime in a crack behind one of the many statues in the Capitol rotunda. *I'll come back for this dime someday,* he told himself, *when I've succeeded.* Fifteen years later the newly elected Congressman David H. Pryor returned to find the dime still in place. Later he told reporters that his experience proves two things—that the dreams of young people should never be underestimated, and that janitors in the Capitol "don't clean the place up much."

David Pryor knew that setting goals is an important life skill. He was willing to commit himself to a plan of action that would take years to complete.

Not all goals, however, are so long-range. Goals can be very useful in going after less important things, too. Whether short- or long-term, a goal is important in getting what you want. It fulfills at least three practical functions.

First, it serves as a road map. In planning how to achieve something, a goal provides the landmarks you'll have to pass to get where you want to go.

Second, it serves as a compass. It gives a sense of direction, keeps you on course, prevents you from being detoured or distracted as you pursue it. If one of your goals is service for Christ, "continue to live in him."

Third, a goal serves as an odometer. It provides a way to measure your progress. It tells you how far you've gone and how far you have to go.

And sometimes it helps to choose some small token as a symbol of your goal. This is what David Pryor was doing when he slipped the dime into the crack behind the statue. If you have a goal in life, invest a dime in it. It will be the best 10 cents you ever spent.

☞ In your own words, state the four steps to a successful relationship with Jesus outlined in Colossians 2:6, 7.

☞ How can you know what is a worthy goal for you to make for yourself?

☞ Invest a dime—literally—in your future. Place it in a symbolic location; give it to someone to return to you at a designated time, etc., so that it will serve as a concrete token of your dedication, with God's help, to achieve a goal.

Day 3

"Love the Lord your God with all your heart and with all your soul and with all your mind.' This is the first and greatest commandment" *(Matt. 22:37, 38, NIV).*

The Parents of the Blind Man

The old man secured the door behind himself
and sagged on the bench.
His wife took care
to light the oil lamp
and then came over to him, frightened.
"Do you think they'll be

bothering us again?" she asked.

He sighed wearily,

his red-rimmed old eyes

blinking in confusion.

"I don't know why they should.

It isn't our fault it happened."

"What do you mean, 'fault'?"

"Now, wife, I didn't mean it that way."

He patted her cheek

the way he always did

when she became ruffled.

"Of course, I'm happy he's been healed,

but the Pharisees think that

we've become disciples too.

Why do we have to be drawn

into all this controversy?" he muttered.

"Our son's old enough

to answer for himself—

as I told them over and over."

The old man ground his fist

into his open palm.

"This Nazarene stirs up turmoil

everywhere he goes.

He does a good work, I suppose,

but I'm too old for all these new ideas.

If we had never heard of him,

we wouldn't be in this trouble.

All I want out of life

is a little peace and quiet."

↪ "All I want out of life is a little peace and quiet." Explain why you agree or disagree that this is a worthy goal.

↪ How can you know when to continue to pursue a goal and when to give up on it?

↪ Write down three goals that you would like to achieve in the next five years. Think about the intermediate steps that you will probably have to take to achieve each of these goals. Ask God's blessing and guidance as you pursue them.

Day 4

"What profit is there if you gain the whole world—and lose eternal life? What can be compared with the value of eternal life?" (Matt. 16:26, TLB).

The Price of a Whistle

When Benjamin Franklin was a child, an adult friend gave him a small amount of change as a gift. Young Ben used all the money to buy a whistle from a playmate. Benjamin played the whistle all over the house. He thoroughly enjoyed his new whistle till someone advised him that he had paid four times what it was worth. Instantly that whistle lost all its value to young Benjamin.

In later years Franklin remembered the bad bargain he had made in buying the whistle from his playmate. Whenever he observed someone sacrificing friendship or family for fame or fortune, he would say, "He pays too much for his whistle."

This is how it was for Judas Iscariot. Whatever his motivation, he betrayed Jesus for worldly gain. Later he realized his dreadful mistake. He took his own life because he knew he had paid too much for his whistle.

With tongue in cheek Garrison Keillor talks about this in *We Are Still Married*: "Someday *Reader's Digest* will print an article about the tiny gland below the kneecap called the hermer that produces a thin golden fluid that enables the brain to feel pleasure: if a person quits the bad habit of crossing his legs, his hermer can recover and life become wonderful. But so far all the *Digest* says is what I already know: drink plenty of liquids. I need to know something more miraculous than that, the secret of happiness. What, as a child, I thought Christmas would give or college or show business, and, as a youth, I thought that sex would give, now, as a man, I am still looking for. I thought I'd find it in my writing, but writing is only work, like auto repair except more professional."

Satan designs the things of this world to be attractive and pleasurable. There is nothing really wrong with wealth and fame unless we have to give Jesus up in the bargain to get them. For a child, like young Benjamin Franklin, a lowly whistle may be the most desirable thing he can think of. As we grow up, however, we tend to become drawn to more sophisticated things. Today we may be attracted to the latest in clothing, music, cars. There is nothing wrong with any of these things in themselves—as long as we don't pay too great a price.

↪ How can we know whether God approves of the goals we set?

↪ What can we do to avoid paying too much for our whistle when it comes to setting and achieving goals? Be specific.

↪ Look up some quotations of Benjamin Franklin. Think about some of these that refer to the setting and achieving of one's goals.

"Now listen, you who say, 'Today or tomorrow we will go to this or that city, spend a year there, carry on business and make money.' Why, you do not even know what will happen tomorrow" (James 4:13, 14, NIV).

The Burning Bush

Jethro's sheep had wandered
    as they often did
    onto one of Horeb's shoulders.
One by one they raised their heads,
    looked intently to the east.
Was something there, or was it not?
At first—dreamlike—
    he thought the sun
        had glinted off the amulet
            of someone in a passing caravan.
But then it grew—
    defined itself—
    flickered and danced seductively—
        blue-white-centered and translucent orange.
And just as he was wondering,
    Could it be the heat
        is playing tricks on me?
    he heard the faintest crackling sound.
Like a single animal,
    the sheep shuddered
        at the scent of smoke.

Who would build a fire so large,

> he wondered,

at this time of day?

Taking up his staff,

> he turned toward it to investigate,
>
> couldn't have it frightening the sheep—
>
> and took his first, unknowing step
>
> > toward the Promised Land.

☞ Explain why you agree or disagree that James 4:13, 14 and "The Burning Bush" disfavor planning for one's future.

☞ How does the practice of faith relate to planning one's future?

☞ Light a candle, and, as you look into the flame, think about Moses' experience with the burning bush. Consider how God communicates His will for your life today.

Day 6

"If you believe, you will receive whatever you ask for in prayer" (Matt. 21:22, NIV).

Mean Mildred

John Forester's heart must have just about stopped when he went to his barn one weekend morning and discovered that a 1,200-pound pregnant moose had decided to take up residence there. Because his property is near Grand Teton National Park in northwestern Wyoming, Forester was used to seeing an occasional moose, but never quite this close. And it looked as though this moose had come to stay. Plenty of water and hay under a covered roof—what more could she ask?

So when Forester tried to get into the barn to feed his horses,

Mean Mildred, as he named her, charged at him and drove him off. He returned with a rifle and fired a couple rounds in the air, but "she turned right around and turned her ears flat and came right at me," he said. He dived into the safety of some nearby bushes.

By Monday morning Forester had to escort his kids to their school bus with a rifle in his hand. So he called the game and fish agency, who sent officer Tom Tillman to see what he could do to get Mean Mildred out of the barn—after all, the horses were getting hungry.

Officer Tillman tried a gun that shoots whistling firecrackers. Mildred wasn't impressed. "I chased her around for a while," Tillman said laughingly, "and then she chased me around for a while. She was pretty aggressive."

Tuesday morning Tillman decided to take more drastic measures. He returned with a tranquilizing gun, but the moose nonchalantly shook off the darts. Then, as the two men discussed further tactics, Mean Mildred leaped up, bolted over the fence, and ran away.

Sometimes a Mean Mildred moves into our lives, an obstacle that prevents us from achieving a goal. Whatever we try to do, nothing seems to work. The obstacle stands tenaciously in our way, and we feel powerless to get by it. But God has promised that whatever Mean Mildreds we may have in our lives, He will help us to overcome them.

↪ What conditions are implicit in the promise of Matthew 21:22?

↪ What kind of Mean Mildred are you facing this week? How can God help you to get by it?

↪ In prayer, ask God to guide you as you seek to set responsible, balanced goals for your life in Him.

"Whether you eat or drink or whatever you do, do it all for the glory of God" (1 Cor. 10:31, NIV).

Making It Personal

Try some of the following activities as you complete this week's consideration of the subject of goals:

↻ Observe a team sporting event and analyze its implications for goal-setting. What are the goals of the athletes involved? How do they attempt to achieve those goals? To what extent are compromise and commitment involved?

↻ From diverse materials, create a collage that expresses the goals you have in life. Be sure to include in this composition symbols for spiritual, mental, social, and physical goals.

↻ Read the chapter "Consecration" in *Steps to Christ*.

↻ Think of three stories from Scripture that deal with the setting of goals. Analyze the role that God plays in the establishment of goals for the characters in these stories.

↻ Imagine that your home is burning down, that all your loved ones are safe, but that you have time to save only five items from your home before it is destroyed. What would these items be? Think about how your choice of what to save reflects your goals.

Miracles

"I will give you a new heart and put a new spirit in you; I will re-move from you your heart of stone and give you a heart of flesh. And I will put my Spirit in you and move you to follow my decrees and be careful to keep my laws" (Eze. 36:26, 27, NIV).

Kicking the Rabbit Habit

"No rabbits?" Lobo said. "You've got to be kidding!"

But Joshua, the new member of the wolf pack, clearly wasn't joking. As a matter of fact, the serious look in his golden-brown eyes showed his sincerity. "I tell you, Lobo," he said with a dis-turbingly authoritative sweep of his tail, "rabbits were never re-ally meant to be eaten by wolves. If you continue a steady diet of such food, you will never be more than you presently are."

"Do I look sickly to you?" Lobo asked sarcastically.

Joshua smiled and looked Lobo over. His fur was thick and lus-trous. His chest swept down, supporting strong, sturdy legs. As the leader of the pack, he obviously had to be in good condition, to know a thing or two about being a wolf. The long, echoing call of his midnight howl brought as many as a dozen wolves out of the ghostly shadows every night. His territory lay over three valleys. And the notion of giving up rabbits seemed self-evidently ludicrous.

"Look, Joshua," Lobo said patiently, "if you want to eat mustard greens and miner's lettuce and mushrooms, you go right ahead. But wolves were meant to hunt rabbits, not rabbit food!"

"That might be OK," Joshua said, "if your goal in life is to remain only a wolf."

It was several days before Lobo thought about the issue again. In fact, he'd forgotten about it almost entirely. "Why didn't you answer my call last night, Joshua? We had a pretty good hunt."

"Oh, I couldn't see any sense in going along if I weren't going to hunt anyway," Joshua said.

"You mean you're still on that nonrabbit thing? I thought you'd have given it up by now."

"Well, I have to admit," Joshua said, "that I still miss the hunt now and then, but I really am beginning to feel noticeably better. And you would too."

"But hunting rabbits is an inherent part of 'wolfness.'"

Joshua looked at Lobo with that half-smile that wolves have, but Lobo sensed that he would not give up so easily. He knew he'd have to come up with better arguments. "Maybe 'wolfness' isn't what life is all about," Joshua said quietly.

As time went on, Lobo himself began to notice that the rabbits they managed to hunt down just didn't bring the satisfaction that he'd been used to. There was some talk around the pack that maybe the territory wasn't large enough to support so many wolves.

Deke, one of the strong, young males, was the most outspoken. "I tell you," he said one evening as the pack was forming on the moonlit crest of a hill, "the rabbits are getting scarcer and scrawnier every day. If we don't do something about it, we'll all be eating miner's lettuce like Joshua."

"We could move on to a new territory," suggested another pack member.

"Well," Lobo said, "giving up the rabbit habit *is* new territory. Maybe it *is* time to reexamine our so-called wolfness."

This left the rest of the pack a little dazed. But in the long, sleepy afternoons, when wolves are lazing around in their dens,

Lobo would roll over in sleepy semiconsciousness and remember what Deke and Joshua had said. *Could it be,* he wondered as he lolled in the afternoon sun, *that I should be eating mustard greens instead?*

Finally the issue came to a head one night when Deke was complaining, as usual. "Well," Lobo said in an offhand manner, "maybe Joshua is on to something. Anybody for miner's lettuce?" He laughed as he said it, but he was testing the opinion of the pack.

"Not me!" Deke said. "I think I'll head up north and see if things are any better up that way. I'll starve if I stay around here. Anybody want to come along?"

"I think I'll see how this nonrabbit thing works out," Lobo said. "Those who've tried it say they never felt better."

"Lobo, you're crazy. It's unnatural. The next thing you know, Joshua will have you climbing trees."

Climbing trees! Lobo thought. *Why not? Who knows for sure where it could all lead?*

↪ In what respects is a spiritually life-changing event a miracle?

↪ "Kicking the Rabbit Habit" is not about what we eat. In a single sentence, explain the central theme of this parable in your own words.

↪ Listen to sounds around you. Think about the effects of sounds on your behavior. To what extent do you affect the sounds around you? To what extent do they affect you?

Day 2

"Remember the wonders he has done, his miracles, and the judgments he pronounced" (Ps. 105:5, NIV).

Astonishing

Two perfect moons—

one just touching the eastern hills,

the other on the tranquil surface

of Galilee—

a handful of shaken fishermen,

abashed at their own faithlessness,

whispering among themselves,

"What manner of man is this?"

a question they could not fully answer

until He was gone.

↷ Define *miracle* in your own words.

↷ Why do you think it appears that miracles are not as apparent today as they were in Bible times?

↷ In a topical Bible, find a list of Jesus' miracles. Which among these do you consider to be the most dramatic? Why?

"If anyone is in Christ, he is a new creation; the old has gone, the new has come!" (2 Cor. 5:17, NIV).

Changing Your DNA

Searching for the perfect gift? Look no further. Here is the absolute answer: a DNA trinket.

Thanks to so-called advances in DNA research, an entrepreneur is now producing jewelry and other products that contain snippets of genetic material from Marilyn Monroe, Abraham Lincoln, John Kennedy, and other people of note. For only $50 to $300, you can carry with you anywhere a small piece of someone whom you have admired.

If you could own a piece of DNA from anyone in human history, whose would it be?

In a way, this is what we do when we accept Jesus into our lives. We take a snippet of His "spiritual DNA," but instead of carrying it around to show off to others, we actually fuse it to our own spiritual DNA. At this point, something exciting happens. We begin the process of becoming more and more like Jesus, of becoming a whole new person.

This is what Paul meant when he said that "if anyone is in Christ, he is a new creation." Truly, when Jesus changes our hearts, He is really changing our spiritual DNA. And that's a gift of immeasurable value.

↻ Compare and contrast "Changing Your DNA" with "Kicking the Rabbit Habit" (see page 124). What do these two articles have to do with the subject of miracles?

↻ What miracles have you observed in your own life?

↻ Interview a scientist you know who is a Christian. Ask him or her to discuss the relationship between science and miracles.

"[Jesus] is able to save completely those who come to God through him, because he always lives to intercede for them" (Heb. 7:25, NIV).

Simon's Mother-in-law

Two women sat
under the silver-leafed olive trees
near the well
and watched the children
playing in the evening's cool.
  "It would be dishonest of me,"
the older one said,
her hair as silver as the olive leaves,
"to say I have always approved
of everything Peter's done.
You know how I am—
everything in its place—
but Peter is something different,
I can tell you.
My daughter married him—
'So be it,' I said,
but I wondered many times how she could put
up with him.
  "And then he began
to follow the carpenter's son—
from Nazareth, of all places.
Peter just dropped his nets one day
and walked away;

fancied he'd become a rabbi
or some such thing.

"Then he began bringing
the Nazarene home with him—
always with the rabble
trailing behind them.
It was a mess, I can tell you,
trying to keep the place in order
and everyone fed.
My daughter and I
surprised each other
when we were captured by him too.
That carpenter's son—
either he was what he said he was,
or he was a charlatan;
everything boiled down to that.

"The miracle only
made it clearer for me
that I'd made the right decision—
that Peter had made the right decision
in bringing him to us."

She noticed for the first time
the mild look of surprise
on the face of the other woman.

"You haven't heard?" she asked.
"Well, let me tell you—
he healed me!

"A fever was burning me up—
hot as a summer wind, it was—

and the carpenter's son touched me.

The fever was gone instantly."

Her wrinkled face smoothed

into a child's smile.

"But even more important—

I felt my life cooler, lighter, cleaner

than it had ever been before."

↪ In what way is salvation a miracle?

↪ How does Simon's mother-in-law broaden the definition of her own miraculous healing?

↪ List five miracles that you would like to ask God for in prayer. Keep this list handy when you pray.

Day 5

"Though evil is sweet in his mouth and he hides it under his tongue, though he cannot bear to let it go and keeps it in his mouth, yet his food will turn sour in his stomach; it will become the venom of serpents within him" (Job 20:12-14, NIV).

Tastes Great—Less Thrilling!

Since Jesus' birth two millennia ago, Christianity has played a significant role in Western culture. Some of its contributions have been deeply inspiring; some, embarrassing; some, downright amusing.

The role of miracles over the past 20 centuries, for example, has been taken seriously by the true believers, but a source of ridicule for others. And when you consider some of the claims that Christians have made regarding the potency of the saints, it doesn't come as a surprise when someone like Erasmus could scoff that one slipper of Thomas à Becket seemed to be more powerful after the saint was dead than his whole body was while he yet lived.

Relics—even so inconsequential an item as a snippet of fingernail or a lock of hair—have been considered by the devout to have incredible power. The story is told of two beggars, one lame and one blind, who happened to get in the way of a procession bearing the relics of Saint Martin. Fearful that if they were healed of their disabilities they would lose their only means of support, the one who could not walk climbed quickly onto the shoulders of the one who could not see, and together they tried to escape the range of the relics' awesome influence, to no avail. Alas, they were both cured.

Whether or not this actually occurred, it offers an amusing picture of humanity when it comes in direct contact with God's power. Sometimes we simply don't want to be helped. As odd as it may seem, we often prefer our lame and blind condition. It must surely make observers on other worlds scratch their heads in wonderment.

Sooner or later, however, we come to realize that our sinful nature isn't as sweet as we at first thought it was. It just plain isn't natural.

↪ In what respects are you superstitious?

↪ In practical terms, how can a person know whether he or she bases any behavior on superstition?

↪ In a library or on the Internet, research the traditions in the medieval Christian church regarding the potency of relics. Consider what these traditions suggest about the faith of the people of that time.

Day 6

"I will astound these people with wonder upon wonder; the wisdom of the wise will perish, the intelligence of the intelligent will vanish" (Isa. 29:14, NIV).

That Was Then . . .

I used to think
> the angels must get pretty bored
>> without the miracles
>> they used to arrange
>> in Bible times—
>>> parting the Red Sea,
>>> closing the lions' mouths,
>>> sneaking Peter out of prison.

Compared to those,
> the simple incidents
>> in missionaries' stories
>>> were small potatoes.

But who's to say
> which are the bigger—
>> the miracles of Palestine,
>> or of Peru and Papua New Guinea?

↪ Why do you think foreign missionaries seem to observe miracles more readily than those who stay home?

↪ How does one evaluate the authenticity of an apparent miracle? Be specific.

↪ Take a walk through your neighborhood. What evidences of the miraculous do you see?

"Jesus did many other miraculous signs in the presence of his disciples, which are not recorded in this book. But these are written that you may believe that Jesus is the Christ, the Son of God, and that by believing you may have life in his name" (John 20:30, 31, NIV).

Making It Personal

Try some of the following activities as you complete this week's consideration of the subject of miracles:

- ↻ Television has recently broadcast several shows that depict the miraculous. Watch one of these programs and compare and contrast it with the Bible's view of miracles.

- ↻ Read the chapter "The True Sign" in *The Desire of Ages.*

- ↻ Draw your own illustration of one of Jesus' miracles. If you feel that you don't have a talent for this kind of expression, imagine that you are an artist and think about the following questions: What are the details that you would include? How would you represent Jesus in relation to the other people in the drawing?

- ↻ With a friend, prepare three vignettes in which you portray in mime three miracles of Jesus. Offer to perform these vignettes for your church family to introduce a discussion of miracles.

- ↻ Imagine that you have been assigned to debate with someone on the topic: Miracles in the New Testament were merely occurrences for which witnesses of the time had no scientific explanation. You are to represent the side of the debate that considers the miracles of the Bible to be supernatural occurrences that were caused by God's power. Outline the major points that you would include in your argument.

Witness

"We have different gifts, according to the grace given us. If a man's gift is prophesying, let him use it in proportion to his faith. If it is serving, let him serve; if it is teaching, let him teach; if it is encouraging, let him encourage; if it is contributing to the needs of others, let him give generously; if it is leadership, let him govern diligently; if it is showing mercy, let him do it cheerfully" (Rom. 12:6-8, NIV).

Two Anglers and Two Angles

Two men walked into a bookstore, looking for something that would be interesting to read, something that would help them in some way to transcend their boring, everyday lives. Though they had never met each other, by coincidence they each bought a copy of the same best-seller and went their separate ways.

Now, as so often happens in such circumstances, these two men, in the bosoms of their respective homes, each sat down on the same evening to read his copy of the best-seller, and each responded to it in a different way. It's funny, sometimes, how two people can read the very same sentence in a book and react to it with amazingly divergent interpretations. Yet a differing of interpretations doesn't necessarily mean that one is wrong or that both are wrong. They're simply different.

So it happened in this situation. During his study each man

came across the same intriguing quotation that went something like this: "I will make you fishermen." And each was instantly captivated in his own way by the startling image of himself in a heroic new role. This was a concept that neither had hitherto considered.

Bright and early the very next morning, the two men set out on an errand that looked as though it were going to head in exactly the same direction. They went to the nearest sporting goods store, still completely oblivious of each other, and each purchased the most outlandish assortment of fishing equipment imaginable: coops and waders and drails and jigs and creels and all manner of esoteric stuff that they just knew they would need but were absolutely clueless as to how exactly it was supposed to be put to use.

Of one thing they were both sure, however, and that was *where* they were supposed to begin their careers as fishermen: where the fish were. That seemed obvious enough. A lively stream dashed and rippled its way through town, and it didn't exactly take a rocket scientist to conclude that this was the likeliest place to become a fisherman.

So it was that on the sandy margins of the stream the two men first became aware of each other. The one was just settling down on a rock on the north bank of the creek when he glanced up and saw the other shuffling down the bank on the south side with much the same kinds of equipment and a strikingly zealous look on his face. They eyed each other suspiciously for a long moment, and then, wordlessly, set to this exciting new task of fishing. As each became engrossed in his own process, they forgot about each other. One slowly gravitated downstream; the other headed gradually upstream.

By the end of the day, as the orange sun was just sinking past the range of hills to the west, the two fishermen returned to the spot in the stream where they'd begun that morning. They regarded each other for a time from opposite sides of the stream, and then, amiably enough, the one on the north shore called to the other, "Did you catch any fish today?"

A quizzical look played across the face of the one on the south shore. "Catch any fish?" he asked. "Whatever do you mean?"

"What have you been doing all day?" North Shore asked. "You're a fisherman, aren't you? Judging from the fine array of gear you have, I assumed as much."

"Well, of course I'm a fisherman," South Shore said, "but I didn't come down here to *catch* fish. I came to the stream to *feed* them."

Now it was North Shore's turn to look confused. "You what?"

"You heard me right," South Shore said. "I feed the fish. That's what a fisherman does. Haven't you read the best-seller?"

"Of course I have," North Shore said. But where did you read that a fisherman is supposed to feed fish?" he asked.

"Well, it's really quite a simple matter of interpretation," South Shore said with an offhand shrug of the shoulders. "It's all there in the best-seller. In one place it tells us that we should become fishermen, and in another it says to 'feed my sheep.' If we're supposed to feed sheep, why shouldn't we also be expected to feed fish? Aren't the two really metaphors for the same thing? Because of the best-seller, I've felt a calling to feed *something*. Why not fish?"

North Shore gaped. This really was a poser. How could someone spend all day fishing and have nothing to show for their efforts—nothing in their creel? He stood there for the longest moment, assimilating this astonishing revelation with just the quiet ripple of the stream whispering past.

"You know," he said at last with a friendly smile, "maybe there's a place for both of our approaches to this fisherman thing."

"Tell you what," South Shore offered. "Perhaps we can complement each other in this effort. "I'll feed them and you catch them."

North Shore nodded. "Fair enough!" he said.

↪ Explain in your own words the connection between Romans 12:6-8 and "Two Anglers and Two Angles."

↪ Do you consider yourself a feeder of fish or a catcher of fish? Explain your answer.

↷ In prayer, ask God to help you discover your own personal witnessing skills and to give you the opportunity to use them to their fullest.

"By the open statement of the truth we commend ourselves to the conscience of everyone in the sight of God" (2 Cor. 4:2, NRSV).

Espionage

Why spies into Jericho?
What was to gain—
location of armories?
estimation of fighting strength?
sabotage?
God was planning conquest
in His own way anyway:
tear the walls down,
leaving Rahab's place
standing ragged at the edges
in the settling dust.
Maybe Rahab was the reason:
the spies were missionaries
with a message like
"Come out of her, my people,"
and Rahab came out—
a prostitute, of all things—
without crossing her doorsill.

↷ What do you think was God's reason for sending the spies into Jericho?

➨ In what respect is today's Christian a spy in Jericho?

➨ Imagine yourself the superior of the 12 spies sent into Jericho. In modern language, write the assignment to infiltrate the city and outline the specific objectives for the mission.

Day 3

"I delight in weaknesses, in insults, in hardships, in persecutions, in difficulties. For when I am weak, then I am strong" (2 Cor. 12:10, NIV).

Uh, No Thanks!

When Brett Calvin was elected mayor of Latham, Kansas, he was less than amused. No one had registered as a candidate for the office. So with Brett's 17 write-in votes—most of them from his own sizable family—it didn't take a large polling firm like Gallup or Yankelovich to project his victory. This groundswell of public sentiment suddenly catapulted him into an unwanted position of leadership.

The problem is that Latham is a small municipality. When the only city employee calls in sick or takes a vacation, Hizzoner the mayor has to step in and perform some of the less glamorous aspects of the job, such as mowing lawns and reading water meters. And what kind of remuneration can he expect for his efforts? Nada! Zip!

Several biblical stories recount similar experiences. Jeremiah protested that he was too young to accept God's mantle of leadership. Elijah voiced his fear of having to face a wrathful king and queen. Moses professed an inability to express himself well. Paul complained that the job was just too difficult for him to handle. Basically, these heroes all came to a point in their lives when they said to God, "Uh, no thanks!"

Of course, it could be pointed out that Brett Calvin wasn't faced with exactly the same challenges that God was asking of the likes of Jeremiah, Elijah, Moses, or Paul. But no reason is justified for turning down God's call to accept some new responsibility. When we undertake a difficult assignment that God sends our way, we won't have to rely on our own strengths to see us through. We can "delight in weakness."

↻ How can someone know with certainty that he or she has had a call from God to do something? Be specific.

↻ Describe a time you've had a chance to "delight in weakness" for something God asked you to do.

↻ List the names of three people you know to whom you have never talked about religion. Prayerfully watch for the Holy Spirit's leading in opportunities to share your faith.

Day 4

"Always be prepared to give an answer to everyone who asks you to give the reason for the hope that you have. But do this with gentleness and respect" (1 Peter 3:15, NIV).

The Child

Breathless and perspiring,
the child rushed into the house.
"I'm sorry I'm late, Mother,
but wait till you hear.
The greatest thing happened!"
"Now, don't come in here," she said,
more in weariness than in reproach,
"and try to put me off
with another of your wild stories."

"This is different, Mother, really different."
His brown eyes widened.
"The Nazarene led us all
to a hill where He
told us to sit down.

"Everybody was getting hungry,
so I gave the Nazarene
my loaves and fishes,
and you know what He did?
He took the basket in His arms
and asked God to bless the food,
and reached into my basket.
He just reached into the basket—
again and again and again—
the food never stopped.
He fed the whole crowd, Mother.
There must have been
a million people there!
The bread and fish
just kept coming and coming.
And when everybody was full,
there were 12 baskets of leftovers!"
He spread out all 10 fingers
and then, realizing they weren't enough,
repeated, "Twelve!"

The child recognized
the way his mother looked at him.
He had seen it before.
"You don't believe me, do you?"

She sighed and shook her head.

"That's all right," he said.

"Someday you will."

↪ In your own words, state "the reason for the hope that you have".

↪ In your opinion, what does it mean to witness "with gentleness and respect"? Be specific.

↪ Talk to a friend about what it means to witness "with gentleness and respect." Think of three ways you and your friend can tell others about Jesus in this way.

Day 5

"You have been my help, and in the shadow of your wings I sing for joy. My soul clings to you; your right hand upholds me" (Ps. 63:7, 8, NRSV).

Where Blessings Come From

Nicknamed the Galloping Ghost, football running back Red Grange was noted for his ability to elude tacklers. In an October 18, 1924, game against the University of Michigan, Grange had one of the greatest days in college football history. After returning the opening kickoff for 95 yards and a touchdown, he scored on runs of 67, 56, and 45 yards—all in the first 12 minutes of the game. Later in the game he ran for a fifth touchdown and threw a pass for a sixth.

One day a reporter asked Grange why he seemed to be able to avoid tackles so easily. "I can't explain it or take credit for it," Grange said. "You can teach a man how to block or tackle, run or pass, but you can't teach a man how to run so tacklers can't tackle him. No one ever taught me, and I can't teach anyone. If you can't explain it, how can you take credit for it?"

Usually, when an athlete answers such a question from the media, he or she offers some human explanation—concentration, hard work, good coaching, whatever. But Red Grange was humble about his abilities. He didn't try to take credit for something that he'd been born with.

King Solomon, the wisest man who ever lived, could have learned something from Red Grange. After achieving such great- ness and leading Israel during its golden era, Solomon forgot where all his blessings had come from. He began to take full credit for his success. And because of that, God had to step in and remind him of his place in the scheme of things.

Whatever the ability—punting a football, solving difficult mathematical formulas, writing beautiful sentences, baking deli- cious cakes, arranging graceful flower displays—it all comes from God. And God should be the one who gets the credit for it.

↪ In what respects is giving God credit for your blessings a form of witnessing?

↪ How can someone give God credit when he or she is compli- mented for doing something well? Be specific.

↪ Find something in your possession that you value greatly. Write a short psalm of thanks to God for giving this to you.

"To the weak I became weak, to win the weak. I have become all things to all men so that by all possible means I might save some" *(1 Cor. 9:22, NIV).*

No Green Thumb

The old man across the street
    saw me coming with my Bible.
The curtains at the window
    quivered like a tremulous eyelid.
He knew I saw him sitting there,
    but my tapping at the door
        was unwelcome and ignored.
So I left my Bible home
    and caught him in his garden—
        his dahlias are the finest on the block—
and I asked him
    what he did to get such blooms.
"My flowers are like people,"
    he said. "It's sometimes best
        not to try to prune them for a while."

↪ In a single sentence, state the relevance of "No Green Thumb" to the subject of witnessing.

↪ How does one develop a "green thumb" for witnessing? Be specific.

↪ List three ways that witnessing is like gardening, and then three ways it is unlike gardening.

Day 7

"Whoever turns a sinner from the error of his way will save him from death and cover over a multitude of sins" (James 5:20, NIV).

Making It Personal

Try some of the following activities as you complete this week's consideration of the subject of witness:

- ↻ Interview someone who is "witnessing" for a political or religious organization other than your own. Ask what role this activity plays in his or her life. How does he or she cope with rejection? Think about the similarities and differences between this kind of witnessing and Christian witnessing.

- ↻ After reviewing "The Child" (see page 140), consider the following: What if Jesus had also furnished a can of soda to everyone who received the loaves and fishes that day? Calculate how many cans that would be. Call a local soft drink bottling company, and ask how many trucks it would take to carry that much soda. Think about what this suggests about the power available to us as we witness to others.

- ↻ Read the chapter "The First Evangelists" in *The Desire of Ages*.

- ↻ As you place a candle in your room, sing the words to the familiar children's song "This Little Light of Mine." Keep the candle in your room as a reminder of your commitment to telling others of Jesus.

- ↻ Create your own personal T-shirt iron-on that expresses God's love for you. Wear the shirt on some occasion when it may arouse interest among those you meet.

Grace

"To each one of us grace has been given" (Eph. 4:7, NIV).

The Toy Story

The old toymaker's shop faced a beautiful square, just across the street from a pretty little garden and a cool, inviting fountain. Though it did not occupy the most commanding place in the village, it was the center of the universe for every child in the surrounding area. Boys and girls who were lucky enough to be sent into town on errands by their parents invariably found some excuse to return by way of the toy shop, to peek in the window at all the magical wonders that were being created inside. And then what tales they would have to tell their brothers and sisters when they returned home. You just had to see it for yourself!

In clear, straightforward lettering, the sign over the door read: "Iam and Son, Makers of Quality Toys." That really said it all. The good-natured proprietor and his earnest, hardworking son were known far and wide for the unexcelled sophistication and variety of toys that together they constructed. Each was a unique, priceless creation, and each was made to do something a little different from the rest. No two were alike.

As in many enterprises, of course, other employees participated in the wondrous accomplishments of the establishment, but their roles included such responsibilities as storage, maintenance, cataloging, inventory—that sort of thing. They were support personnel. Yet they were perfectly happy in their work because it was simply awe-inspiring to be a part, however menial, of the most exciting business in the village. Those who worked under the same roof as Iam and Son were considered to be very fortunate indeed.

But then one day (no one knows exactly how the idea originated) one of the employees became disgruntled. He didn't recognize it at first, but it was an unexpectedly dark and evil thought, and he refused to put it out of his mind. All this innovation and creativity was going on around him every day, and he somehow got the notion that he should have been more directly involved in research and development. *Why can't I,* he wondered, *get a little of the admiration and respect of the villagers that the toymaker and his son enjoy?*

The kindly toymaker knew right from the beginning what was going on in the disgruntled worker's mind. It was plain in his behavior that he was growing more and more dissatisfied. Some have said in retrospect that management should have immediately sacked the malcontent, but eventually about a third of the workforce sided with him and had to be forcibly expelled from the premises before order was restored.

And then, a short time later, it became tragically apparent that the toys *themselves* had somehow been infected with the rebellious ideas of the ousted employees. The villagers looked at one another and wondered how this could have come about. Whoever heard of such a thing? Outwardly the toy shop was still the fascinating focus of attention for all the children in the village, but inside it was just short of outright chaos. Dolls were admiring themselves in the mirror without any memory of where their beauty had come from. Puppets were severing their strings and conducting themselves in shocking, unpuppetlike ways. Teddy bears and rocking horses were completely overcome by something called "the law of the jungle." Tin soldiers were choosing up sides and simply annihilating one another.

At this point the villagers thought that surely the toymaker would put his foot down and take drastic measures—burn the place to the ground and start all over. "The best thing he could do," they said, "would be to wash his hands of the whole problem."

The firm of Iam and Son did indeed take drastic measures, but no one in his wildest dreams could have anticipated their corporate strategy. Such was their love for the toys that they adopted an astonishing solution: the toymaker's son would himself *become forever* a toy. As such, he would have to demonstrate the original plan for the creations in the toy shop. Then, if any of them responded to this unparalleled resolution, they could be made new and wouldn't have to suffer the natural consequences of the chaos in the toy shop.

The villagers were horrified. What if the toymaker's son failed to survive the effects of becoming a mere toy? He would be vulnerable to all the mayhem that the toys had brought on themselves.

With grim fascination the villagers have been observing to this day the ordeal of the toymaker's son. Conditions in the shop have gone from bad to worse. Yet through it all, even the most casual observer has come to realize that the toymaker's plan to reorganize—and save—the whole business was the only way to prevent its self-destruction.

↳ In terms fitting the "The Toy Story," how would you define grace?

↳ From a human standpoint, why is demonstrating God's grace to others so difficult?

↳ List three practical ways you can demonstrate God's grace to those around you in the coming week.

Day 2

"When we were utterly helpless with no way of escape, Christ came at just the right time and died for us sinners who had no use for him" (Rom. 5:6, TLB).

Sand

Sift it through your fingers

and count the single grains

as though they were the spinning worlds

in your own created universe.

Could you love the molecule

that scrabbled on the surface

of a single grain of sand—

even if you fathered it yourself?

Perhaps you could

(at least a bit)

if it looked at all like you

and somehow could respond in kind.

But what if it had heard of you

and simply didn't care?

↪ In your own words, explain what is meant by the words "if it . . . somehow could respond in kind."

↪ What is especially ironic about the last two lines of the poem "Sand"?

↪ Think about the most dramatic example of grace you have personally witnessed another human being in his or her treatment of another. What does this suggest about God?

"There is no one righteous, not even one" (Rom. 3:10, NIV).

Gulp!

Eighteen-year-old Brandon Hughes made his appearance in a Memphis, Tennessee, court, as directed, to contest a charge against him for driving with a suspended license and violating vehicle registration laws. He seethed with indignation that he should be summoned to answer for such a thing; his attorney had advised him of his rights under the law. When the time came for Brandon to be sworn in, he rose to his feet and raised his right hand—and a packet of cocaine fell out of his pocket, landing for all to see on the courtroom floor.

Suddenly the traffic violation lost its significance. Witnesses included his lawyer, a police officer, a deputy, and even the presiding judge. Whether or not Brandon Hughes was guilty of driving with a suspended license, under the law his possession of cocaine betrayed a far more serious condition.

In the court of God's judgment it would be best for us to keep in mind the difference between an act and a condition. People may think they will be able to face the final judgment without the evidence of any flaws in their record—no adultery, no murder, no false testimony, no stealing, etc. But from the human standpoint there is no cause for "self"-assurance.

In God's courtroom the judge has witnessed our every act, *and* He can actually read the condition of our hearts. "There is no one righteous, not even one" (Rom. 3:10, NIV).

Two possible conclusions are equally erroneous in God's courtroom: to consider ourselves good enough to be set free, or to conclude in despair that we are without hope. To be saved from such a dilemma all we can do is plead guilty and throw ourselves on the mercy of the court. If we do that, the penalty has already been paid.

↪ What similarities do you see between humankind and Brandon Hughes?

↪ Compare "Gulp!" with "The Toy Story." According to "The Toy Story," how has the penalty "already been paid"?

↪ Write a letter or e-mail message to someone who needs you to demonstrate God's grace to him or her. Offer forgiveness and reconciliation.

Day 4

"Whatever I am now it is all because God poured out such kindness and grace upon me" (1 Cor. 15:10, TLB).

Malchus

In the flickering torchlight,

Malchus looked down into the pool—

black as oil—

where his face wiggled

on the surface of the water.

His brother sat on the pool's edge,

saying nothing, only listening.

"We went out," Malchus continued,

"to Gethsemane tonight

to arrest the Nazarene—

you know, the one John's been following

all over the place."

He ran his finger

over the folds of his ear.

"And a burly fisherman

pulled out a sword—
I don't know if it was his
or someone else's—
and flailed it around
as though he'd take the whole crowd on.

    "I ducked, like this,"
he said, jerking his head to the side,
"and the sword must have grazed my ear.
There wasn't any pain.
I thought he'd missed me—
till I felt the blood
dripping on my shoulder."

    Turning his back on the pool,
he sat down on the curbing
next to his brother.

    "You can see for yourself;
the blood's still there."

    Again his fingers probed his ear.
He pulled at it,
squeezed it till it hurt.

    "It was gone—completely gone!
When they'd subdued the fisherman—
it took six of them to do it—
the Nazarene stooped down
and picked up the ear
and fitted it somehow
back where it belongs.
And when He touched me,
I think I felt—

now I know—

what John's been bleating about

for the past three years."

    His brother made to turn away;

Malchus grasped his arm.

    "I know how it all sounds," he said.

His eyes flared up

brighter than the torchlight.

    "But all I can say is,

'You really couldn't understand

till He's touched you.'"

↪ In spiritual terms, what is meant by the sentence "You really couldn't understand till He's touched you"?

↪ How are God's grace and God's healing the same? How are they different?

↪ Look up the word *grace* in a dictionary and a thesaurus. What other words are related to this important word?

Day 5

"All spoke well of him and were amazed at the gracious words that came from his lips. 'Isn't this Joseph's son?' they asked. Jesus said to them, 'Surely you will quote this proverb to me: "Physician, heal yourself! Do here in your hometown what we have heard that you did in Capernaum." I tell you the truth,' he continued, 'no prophet is accepted in his hometown'" (Luke 4:22-24, NIV).

My Cup Runneth Around

The Stanley Cup—the National Hockey League's most prestigious award—is the oldest professional sports team trophy in

North America. It makes the Super Bowl trophy look like something out of a Cracker Jack box.

Sir Frederick Arthur Stanley, Governor-general of Canada, commissioned the making of the cup back in 1893 for $48.67 (Canadian), but since that time it has become priceless, the goal for thousands of young hockey players throughout the world.

But as revered as the Stanley Cup is, it hasn't always been treated with the utmost respect. In fact, there have been times when it was in danger of being lost or destroyed.

● In 1903 when one of the members of the Ottawa Silver Seven, that year's winning team, took the cup home with him, his teammates found out. In the ensuing fight, the cup got tossed into a cemetery.

● A member of the 1910 Montreal Wanderers placed the cup in the window of his bowling alley, filling it with chewing gum.

● The 1924 Montreal Canadiens were taking the cup with them to the party where they were going to celebrate their victory when they had to get out of the car to fix a flat tire. When they got to the party, they realized they had left the cup on the curb.

Sometimes we lose sight of the value of things simply because we see them every day. We begin to take them for granted. Or we tend to place value on things at least in part because they are so *unfamiliar* to us. An old saying goes, "Familiarity breeds contempt." This is the reasoning behind Jesus' statement that "no prophet is accepted in his hometown."

Sometimes Christians themselves forget just how wonderful was Jesus' sacrifice for us. They begin to take it for granted. But fortunately for us, Jesus' love never flags. He is always there when we return to Him.

"Weak as we are," writes Frederick Buechner in *A Room Called Remember*, "a strength beyond our strength has pulled us through at least this far, at least to this day. Foolish as we are, a wisdom beyond our wisdom has flickered up just often enough to light us if not to the right path through forest, at least to a path that leads forward, that is bearable. Faint of heart as we are, a love beyond our power to love has kept out hearts alive."

↪ In what ways have you personally observed that "no prophet is accepted in his hometown"?

↪ How can a Christian avoid the possibility that Jesus' grace would become too "familiar"? Be specific.

↪ As you watch the sun go down some evening, think about the specific examples of God's grace that you have experienced that day.

Day 6

"It is not the one who commends himself who is approved, but the one whom the Lord commends" (2 Cor. 10:18, NIV).

Chore, or More?

Once there was a boy

who washed the dishes

and cleaned his room for a week

and then asked his father

for a dollar.

"Don't you think I've earned it?"

he asked with a smile.

But his father shook his head.

"You can't earn anything

by keeping your room clean," he said.

"That's in your own best interest, after all.

Do it because you love me—

and because you love yourself."

And when the boy
switched his emphasis
and mowed the lawn
because it needed it
and because it spared
his father the work,
his father graced him with a reward
far greater than a dollar.

↻ What scriptural support is there for the idea that good works should result "because you love me—and because you love yourself"?

↻ In what ways have you done good things for the wrong reasons? Be specific.

↻ Think about one of the scriptural references in this week's readings. Prayerfully consider how this verse can bring you into a greater appreciation for God's grace in your life.

Day 7

"Let us then approach the throne of grace with confidence, so that we may receive mercy and find grace to help us in our time of need" (Heb. 4:16, NIV).

Making It Personal

Try some of the following activities as you complete this week's consideration of the subject of grace:

↻ Think of three examples of God's grace as it is illustrated in object lessons from nature. Prepare to share one of these examples in a short presentation for children.

↻ Research the background to the hymn "Amazing Grace." Then as you listen to a recording of it on cassette or CD, think about the unmerited favor you have received from God in your life.

↻ In some art form (drawing, painting, sculpture, etc.), produce your own portrayal of grace.

↻ Read the chapter "The Measure of Forgiveness" in *Christ's Object Lessons.*

↻ Write a job description for God, in which you state His most important traits of character. Think about how grace would figure in such a job description.